CONTENTS

CONTENTS

ARISTOTLE, *PHYSICS*, Book II, Chapters 1, 2, 3, 7, 8
Adapted from the public domain English translation by
R.P. Hardie and R.K. Gaye

*The first six paragraphs of Chapter 3 are required
reading for all sections.*

Chapter 1

Of things that exist, some exist by nature, some from other
causes.

'By nature' the animals and their parts exist, and the plants
and the simple bodies (earth, fire, air, water)—for we say
that these and the like exist 'by nature'.

All the things mentioned present a feature in which they
differ from things which are not constituted by nature.
Each of them has within itself a principle of motion and of
stationariness (in respect of place, or of growth and
decrease, or by way of alteration). On the other hand, a bed
and a coat and anything else of that sort, qua receiving
these designations—i.e., in so far as they are products of
art—have no innate impulse to change. But in so far as
they happen to be composed of stone or of earth or of a
mixture of the two, they do have such an impulse, and just
to that extent which seems to indicate that nature is a
source or cause of being moved and of being at rest in that
to which it belongs primarily, in virtue of itself and not in
virtue of a concomitant attribute.

I say 'not in virtue of a concomitant attribute', because (for
instance) a man who is a doctor might cure himself.
Nevertheless it is not in so far as he is a patient that he
possesses the art of medicine: it merely has happened that
the same man is doctor and patient—and that is why these
attributes are not always found together. So it is with all
other artificial products. None of them has in itself the
source of its own production. But while in some cases (for

instance houses and the other products of manual labour) that principle is in something else external to the thing, in other—those which may cause a change in themselves in virtue of a concomitant attribute—it lies in the things themselves (but not in virtue of what they are).

'Nature' then is what has been stated. Things 'have a nature' which have a principle of this kind. Each of them is a substance; for it is a subject, and nature always implies a subject in which it inheres.

The term 'according to nature' is applied to all these things and also to the attributes which belong to them in virtue of what they are, for instance the property of fire to be carried upwards—which is not a 'nature' nor 'has a nature' but is 'by nature' or 'according to nature'.

What nature is, then, and the meaning of the terms 'by nature' and 'according to nature', has been stated. That nature exists, it would be absurd to try to prove; for it is obvious that there are many things of this kind, and to prove what is obvious by what is not is the mark of a man who is unable to distinguish what is self-evident from what is not. (This state of mind is clearly possible. A man blind from birth might reason about colours. Presumably therefore such persons must be talking about words without any thought to correspond.)

Some identify the nature or substance of a natural object with that immediate constituent of it which taken by itself is without arrangement, e.g., the wood is the 'nature' of the bed, and the bronze the 'nature' of the statue.

As an indication of this Antiphon points out that if you planted a bed and the rotting wood acquired the power of sending up a shoot, it would not be a bed that would come up, but wood—which shows that the arrangement in accordance with the rules of the art is merely an incidental attribute, whereas the real nature is the other, which, further, persists continuously through the process of making.

But if the material of each of these objects has itself the same relation to something else, say bronze (or gold) to water, bones (or wood) to earth and so on, that (they say) would be their nature and essence. Consequently some assert earth, others fire or air or water or some or all of these, to be the nature of the things that are. For whatever any one of them supposed to have this character—whether one thing or more than one thing—this or these he declared to be the whole of substance, all else being its affections, states, or dispositions. Every such thing they held to be eternal (for it could not pass into anything else), but other things to come into being and cease to be times without number.

This then is one account of 'nature', namely that it is the immediate material substratum of things which have in themselves a principle of motion or change.

Another account is that 'nature' is the shape or form which is specified in the definition of the thing.

For the word 'nature' is applied to what is according to nature and the natural in the same way as 'art' is applied to what is artistic or a work of art. We should not say in the latter case that there is anything artistic about a thing, if it is a bed only potentially, not yet having the form of a bed; nor should we call it a work of art. The same is true of natural compounds. What is potentially flesh or bone has not yet its own 'nature,' and does not exist until it receives the form specified in the definition, which we name in defining what flesh or bone is. Thus in the second sense of 'nature' it would be the shape or form (not separable except in statement) of things which have in themselves a source of motion. (The combination of the two, e.g., man, is not 'nature' but 'by nature' or 'natural.')

The form indeed is 'nature' rather than the matter; for a thing is more properly said to be what it is when it has attained to fulfilment than when it exists potentially. Again man is born from man, but not bed from bed. That is why people say that the figure is not the nature of a bed, but the wood is—if the bed sprouted, not a bed but wood would come up. But even if the figure is art, then on the same principle the shape of man is his nature. For man is born from man.

We also speak of a thing's nature as being exhibited in the process of growth by which its nature is attained. The 'nature' in this sense is not like 'doctoring,' which leads not to the art of doctoring but to health. Doctoring must start from the art, not lead to it. But it is not in this way that nature (in the one sense) is related to nature (in the other). What grows qua growing grows from something into something. Into what then does it grow? Not into that from which it arose but into that to which it tends. The shape then is nature.

'Shape' and 'nature,' it should be added, are in two senses. For the privation too is in a way form. But whether in unqualified coming to be there is privation, i.e., a contrary to what comes to be, we must consider later.

Chapter 2

We have distinguished, then, the different ways in which the term 'nature' is used.

The next point to consider is how the mathematician differs from the physicist. Obviously physical bodies contain surfaces and volumes, lines and points, and these are the subject-matter of mathematics.

Further, is astronomy different from physics or a department of it? It seems absurd that the physicist should be supposed to know the nature of sun or moon, but not to know any of their essential attributes, particularly as the writers on physics obviously do discuss their shape also and whether the earth and the world are spherical or not.

Now the mathematician, though he too treats of these things, nevertheless does not treat of them as the limits of a physical body; nor does he consider the attributes indicated as the attributes of such bodies. That is why he separates them; for in thought they are separable from motion, and it makes no difference, nor does any falsity result, if they are separated. The holders of the theory of Forms do the same, though they are not aware of it; for they separate the objects of physics, which are less separable than those of mathematics. This becomes plain if one tries to state in each of the two cases the definitions of the things and of their attributes. 'Odd' and 'even', 'straight' and 'curved', and likewise 'number', 'line', and 'figure', do not involve motion; not so 'flesh' and 'bone' and 'man'—these are defined like 'snub nose', not like 'curved'.

Similar evidence is supplied by the more physical of the branches of mathematics, such as optics, harmonics, and astronomy. These are in a way the converse of geometry. While geometry investigates physical lines but not qua physical, optics investigates mathematical lines, but qua physical, not qua mathematical.

Since 'nature' has two senses, the form and the matter, we must investigate its objects as we would the essence of snubness. That is, such things are neither independent of matter nor can be defined in terms of matter only. Here too indeed one might raise a difficulty. Since there are two natures, with which is the physicist concerned? Or should he investigate the combination of the two? But if the combination of the two, then also each severally. Does it belong then to the same or to different sciences to know each severally?

If we look at the ancients, physics would seem to be concerned with matter. (It was only very slightly that Empedocles and Democritus touched on the forms and the essence.)

But if on the other hand art imitates nature, and it is the part of the same discipline to know the form and the matter up to a point (e.g., the doctor has a knowledge of health and also of bile and phlegm, in which health is realized, and the builder has a knowledge both of the form of the house and of the matter, namely that it is bricks and beams, and so forth): if this is so, it would be the part of physics also to know nature in both its senses.

Again, 'that for the sake of which', or the end, belongs to the same department of knowledge as the means. But the nature is the end or 'that for the sake of which'. For if a thing undergoes a continuous change and there is a stage which is last, this stage is the end or 'that for the sake of which'. (That is why the poet was carried away into making an absurd statement when he said 'he has the end for the sake of which he was born'. For not every stage that is last claims to be an end, but only that which is best.)

For the arts make their material (some simply 'make' it, others make it serviceable), and we use everything as if it were there for our sake. (We also are in a sense an end. 'That for the sake of which' has two senses: the distinction is made in our work *On Philosophy*.) The arts, therefore, which govern the matter and have knowledge are two, namely the art which uses the product and the art which directs the production of it. That is why the using art also is in a sense directive; but it differs in that it knows the form, whereas the art which is directive as being concerned with production knows the matter. For the helmsman knows and prescribes what sort of form a helm should have, the other from what wood it should be made and by means of what operations. In the products of art, however, we make the material with a view to the function, whereas in the products of nature the matter is there all along.

Again, matter is a relative term: to each form there corresponds a special matter. How far then must the physicist know the form or essence? Up to a point, perhaps, as the doctor must know sinew or the smith bronze (i.e., until he understands the purpose of each): and the physicist is concerned only with things whose forms are separable indeed, but do not exist apart from matter. Man is begotten by man and by the sun as well. The mode of existence and essence of the separable it is the business of the primary type of philosophy to define.

Chapter 3

Now that we have established these distinctions, we must proceed to consider causes, their character and number. Knowledge is the object of our inquiry, and men do not think they know a thing till they have grasped the 'why' of it (which is to grasp its primary cause). So clearly we too must do this as regards both coming to be and passing away and every kind of physical change, in order that, knowing their principles, we may try to refer each of our problems to these principles.

In one sense, then, (1) that out of which a thing comes to be and which persists, is called 'cause', e.g., the bronze of the statue, the silver of the bowl, and the genera of which the bronze and the silver are species.

In another sense (2) the form or the archetype, i.e., the statement of the essence, and its genera, are called 'causes' (e.g., of the octave the relation of 2:1, and generally number), and the parts in the definition.

Again (3) the primary source of the change or coming to rest; e.g., the man who gave advice is a cause, the father is cause of the child, and generally *what makes* is the cause of *what is made* and *what causes change* is the cause of *what is changed*.

Again (4) in the sense of end or 'that for the sake of which' a thing is done, e.g., health is the cause of walking about. ('Why is he walking about?' we say. 'To be healthy,' and, having said that, we think we have assigned the cause.) The same is true also of all the intermediate steps which are brought about through the action of something else as means towards the end, e.g., reduction of flesh, purging, drugs, or surgical instruments are means towards

health. All these things are 'for the sake of' the end, though they differ from one another in that some are activities, others instruments.

This then perhaps exhausts the number of ways in which the term 'cause' is used.

As the word has several senses, it follows that there are several causes of the same thing (not merely in virtue of a concomitant attribute), e.g. both the art of the sculptor and the bronze are causes of the statue. These are causes of the statue qua statue, not in virtue of anything else that it may be—only not in the same way, the one being the material cause, the other the cause whence the motion comes. Some things cause each other reciprocally, e.g., hard work causes fitness and vice versa, but again not in the same way, but the one as end, the other as the origin of change. Further the same thing is the cause of contrary results. For that which by its presence brings about one result is sometimes blamed for bringing about the contrary by its absence. Thus we ascribe the wreck of a ship to the absence of the pilot whose presence was the cause of its safety.

All the causes now mentioned fall into four familiar divisions. The letters are the causes of syllables, the material of artificial products, fire, etc., of bodies, the parts of the whole, and the premisses of the conclusion, in the sense of 'that from which'. Of these pairs the one set are causes in the sense of substratum, e.g., the parts, the other set in the sense of essence—the whole and the combination and the form. But the seed and the doctor and the adviser, and generally the maker, are all sources whence the change or stationariness originates, while the others are causes in the sense of the end or the good of the rest; for 'that for the sake of which' means what is best and the end of the things that lead up to it. (Whether we say the 'good itself' or the 'apparent good' makes no difference.)

Such then is the number and nature of the kinds of cause.

Now the modes of causation are many, though when brought under heads they too can be reduced in number. For 'cause' is used in many senses and even within the same kind one may be prior to another (e.g., the doctor and the expert are causes of health, the relation 2:1 and number of the octave), and always what is inclusive to what is particular. Another mode of causation is the incidental and its genera, e.g., in one way 'Polyclitus', in another 'sculptor' is the cause of a statue, because 'being Polyclitus' and 'sculptor' are incidentally conjoined. Also the classes in which the incidental attribute is included; thus 'a man' could be said to be the cause of a statue or, generally, 'a living creature'. An incidental attribute too may be more or less remote, e.g., suppose that 'a pale man' or 'a musical man' were said to be the cause of the statue.

All causes, both proper and incidental, may be spoken of either as potential or as actual; e.g., the cause of a house being built is either 'house-builder' or 'house-builder building'.

Similar distinctions can be made in the things of which the causes are causes, e.g., of 'this statue' or of 'statue' or of 'image' generally, of 'this bronze' or of 'bronze' or of 'material' generally. So too with the incidental attributes. Again we may use a complex expression for either and say, e.g., neither 'Polyclitus' nor 'sculptor' but 'Polyclitus, sculptor'.

All these various uses, however, come to six in number, under each of which again the usage is twofold. Cause means either what is particular or a genus, or an incidental attribute or a genus of that, and these either as a complex or each by itself; and all six either as actual or as potential. The difference is this much, that causes which are actually at work and particular exist and cease to exist simultaneously with their effect, e.g., this healing person with this being-healed person and that house-building man with that being-built house; but this is not always true of potential causes—the house and the housebuilder do not pass away simultaneously.

In investigating the cause of each thing it is always necessary to seek what is most precise (as also in other things): thus man builds because he is a builder, and a builder builds in virtue of his art of building. This last cause then is prior: and so generally.

Further, generic effects should be assigned to generic causes, particular effects to particular causes, e.g., statue to sculptor, this statue to this sculptor; and powers are relative to possible effects, actually operating causes to things which are actually being effected.

This must suffice for our account of the number of causes and the modes of causation.

...

Chapter 7

It is clear then that there are causes, and that the number of them is what we have stated. The number is the same as that of the things comprehended under the question 'why'. The 'why' is referred ultimately either (1), in things which do not involve motion, e.g., in mathematics, to the 'what' (to the definition of 'straight line' or 'commensurable', &c.), or (2) to what initiated a motion, e.g., 'why did they go to war?—because there had been a raid'; or (3) we are inquiring 'for the sake of what?'—'that they may rule'; or (4), in the case of things that come into being, we are looking for the matter. The causes, therefore, are these and so many in number.

Now, the causes being four, it is the business of the physicist to know about them all, and if he refers his problems back to all of them, he will assign the 'why' in the way proper to his science—the matter, the form, the mover, 'that for the sake of which'. The last three often coincide; for the 'what' and 'that for the sake of which' are one, while the primary source of motion is the same in species as these (for man generates man), and so too, in general, are all things which cause movement by being themselves moved; and such as are not of this kind are no longer inside the province of physics, for they cause motion not by possessing motion or a source of motion in themselves, but being themselves incapable of motion. Hence there are three branches of study, one of things which are incapable of motion, the second of things in motion, but indestructible, the third of destructible things.

The question 'why', then, is answered by reference to the matter, to the form, and to the primary moving cause. For in respect of coming to be it is mostly in this last way that causes are investigated—'what comes to be after what? what was the primary agent or patient?' and so at each step of the series.

Now the principles which cause motion in a physical way are two, of which one is not physical, as it has no principle of motion in itself. Of this kind is whatever causes movement, not being itself moved, such as (1) that which is completely unchangeable, the primary reality, and (2) the essence of that which is coming to be, i.e., the form; for this is the end or 'that for the sake of which'. Hence since nature is for the sake of something, we must know this cause also. We must explain the 'why' in all the senses of the term, namely, (1) that from this that will necessarily result ('from this' either without qualification or in most cases); (2) that 'this must be so if that is to be so' (as the conclusion presupposes the premises); (3) that this was the essence of the thing; and (4) because it is better thus (not without qualification, but with reference to the essential nature in each case).

Chapter 8

We must explain then (1) that Nature belongs to the class of causes which act for the sake of something; (2) about the necessary and its place in physical problems, for all writers ascribe things to this cause, arguing that since the hot and the cold, etc., are of such and such a kind, therefore certain things necessarily are and come to be—and if they mention any other cause (one his 'friendship and strife', another his 'mind'), it is only to touch on it, and then good-bye to it.

A difficulty presents itself: why should not nature work, not for the sake of something, nor because it is better so, but just as the sky rains, not in order to make the corn grow, but of necessity? What is drawn up must cool, and what has been cooled must become water and descend, the result of this being that the corn grows. Similarly if a man's crop is spoiled on the threshing-floor, the rain did not fall for the sake of this—in order that the crop might be spoiled—but that result just followed. Why then should it not be the same with the parts in nature, e.g., that our teeth should come up of necessity—the front teeth sharp, fitted for tearing, the molars broad and useful for grinding down the food—since they did not arise for this end, but it was merely a coincident result; and so with all other parts in which we suppose that there is purpose? Wherever then all the parts came about just what they would have been if they had come be for an end, such things survived, being organized spontaneously in a fitting way; whereas those which grew otherwise perished and continue to perish, as Empedocles says his 'man-faced ox-progeny' did.

Such are the arguments (and others of the kind) which may cause difficulty on this point. Yet it is impossible that this should be the true view. For teeth and all other natural things either invariably or normally come about in a given way; but of not one of the results of chance or spontaneity is this true. We do not ascribe to chance or mere coincidence the frequency of rain in winter, but frequent rain in summer we do; nor heat in the dog-days, but only if we have it in winter. If then, it is agreed that things are either the result of coincidence or for an end, and these cannot be the result of coincidence or spontaneity, it follows that they must be for an end; and that such things are all due to nature even the champions of the theory which is before us would agree. Therefore action for an end is present in things which come to be and are by nature.

Further, where a series has a completion, all the preceding steps are for the sake of that. Now surely as in intelligent action, so in nature; and as in nature, so it is in each action, if nothing interferes. Now intelligent action is for the sake of an end; therefore the nature of things also is so. Thus if a house, e.g., had been a thing made by nature, it would have been made in the same way as it is now by art; and if things made by nature were made also by art, they would come to be in the same way as by nature. Each step then in the series is for the sake of the next; and generally art partly completes what nature cannot bring to a finish, and partly imitates her. If, therefore, artificial products are for the sake of an end, so clearly also are natural products. The relation of the later to the earlier terms of the series is the same in both. This is most obvious in the animals other than man: they make things neither by art nor after inquiry or deliberation. Wherefore people discuss whether it is by intelligence or by some other faculty that these creatures work—spiders, ants, and the like. By gradual advance in this direction we come to see clearly that in plants too that is produced which is conducive to the end—leaves, e.g., grow to provide shade for the fruit. If then it is both by nature and for an end that the swallow makes its nest and the spider its web, and plants grow leaves for the sake of the fruit and send their roots down (not up) for the sake of nourishment, it is plain that this kind of cause is operative in things which come to be and are by nature. And since 'nature' means two things, the matter and the form, of which the latter is the end, and since all the rest is for the sake of the end, the form must be the cause in the sense of 'that for the sake of which'.

Now mistakes come to pass even in the operations of art: the grammarian makes a mistake in writing and the doctor pours out the wrong dose. Hence clearly mistakes are possible in the operations of nature also. If then in art there are cases in which what is rightly produced serves a purpose, and if where mistakes occur there was a purpose in what was attempted, only it was not attained, so must it be also in natural products, and monstrosities will be failures in the purposive effort. Thus in the original combinations the 'ox-progeny' if they failed to reach a determinate end must have arisen through the corruption of some principle corresponding to what is now the seed.

Further, seed must have come into being first, and not straightway the animals: the words 'whole-natured first...' must have meant seed.

Again, in plants too we find the relation of means to end, though the degree of organization is less. Were there then in plants also 'olive-headed vine-progeny', like the 'man-headed ox-progeny', or not? An absurd suggestion; yet there must have been, if there were such things among animals.

Moreover, among the seeds anything must have come to be at random. But the person who asserts this entirely does away with 'nature' and what exists 'by nature'. For those things are natural which, by a continuous movement originated from an internal principle, arrive at some completion: the same completion is not reached from every principle; nor any chance completion, but always the tendency in each is towards the same end, if there is no impediment.

The end and the means towards it may come about by chance. We say, for instance, that a stranger has come by chance, paid the ransom, and gone away, when he does so as if he had come for that purpose, though it was not for that that he came. This is incidental, for chance is an incidental cause, as I remarked before. But when an event takes place always or for the most part, it is not incidental or by chance. In natural products the sequence is invariable, if there is no impediment.

It is absurd to suppose that purpose is not present because we do not observe the agent deliberating. Art does not deliberate. If the ship-building art were in the wood, it would produce the same results by nature. If, therefore, purpose is present in art, it is present also in nature. The best illustration is a doctor doctoring himself: nature is like that.

It is plain then that nature is a cause, a cause that operates for a purpose.

COMMENTARY ON THE SENTENCES

QUESTION I

Article 1

5 **Is another doctrine beyond the natural disciplines necessary for men?**

We proceed to the first question thus:

1. It seems that no doctrine beyond the natural disciplines is necessary for man. For as Dionysius says in the Letter to
10 Polycarp, 'Philosophy is the knowledge of the things that exist.' And he observes, making an induction from each of them, that every kind of existing thing is treated in philosophy—of Creator and creature, of the works of nature as well as our works. But any doctrine must be of existing things, since there
15 is no science of non-being. Therefore, there should be no doctrine beside the natural disciplines.

2. Again, every doctrine is for the sake of perfection, either of understanding, as with the speculative intellect, or with respect to an effect issuing in a work, as with the practical
20 intellect. But both are accomplished by philosophy, because intellect is perfected by the demonstrative sciences, and the affections by the moral sciences. Therefore no other doctrine is necessary.

3. Moreover, whatever can be known from the principles
25 of reason by the natural intellect is either treated in, or can be discovered by, the principles of philosophy. But the knowledge that can be achieved by natural intellect suffices for the perfection of man. Therefore, no other science than the philosophical is necessary.

In proof of the middle: That which can achieve its perfection by itself is more noble than that which cannot. But other animals and insensible creatures achieve their ends by purely natural means, though not without God, who works in
5 all things. Therefore man, since he is nobler than they, can acquire knowledge sufficient for his perfection through natural intellect.

ON THE CONTRARY: Hebrews 11: 6: 'Without faith it is impossible to please God.' But it is of the highest necessity to
10 please God. Therefore, since philosophy is incapable of attaining what is of faith, a doctrine which proceeds from the principles of faith is necessary.

Again, an effect which is not proportionate to its cause, leads only imperfectly to knowledge of the cause. All creatures
15 are such an effect with respect to the creator, from whom they are infinitely distant. Therefore, they imperfectly lead to knowledge of him. Since philosophy proceeds from notions derived from creatures, it is insufficient to make God known. Therefore, there must be another higher science, which
20 proceeds from revelation, and makes up for the defect of philosophy.

SOLUTION: For light on this it should be known that all right-thinking men make contemplation of God the end of human life. But there are two kinds of contemplation. The one
25 is through creatures and is imperfect, for the reason already given. Aristotle locates happiness in this kind of contemplation (*Ethics* 10)—it is a happiness on the way', of this life. To it is ordered the whole of philosophical knowledge which proceeds from concepts of creatures. The other is the contemplation of
30 God whereby he is seen immediately in his essence. This is perfect and will be had in the Fatherland and is possible to man on the supposition of faith. Hence it is necessary that the things which are for the sake of the end be proportioned to the end, since a man while on the way is led by the hand to that
35 contemplation, not through knowledge drawn from creatures, but rather as immediately inspired by the divine light. This is the doctrine of theology.

From this we can draw two conclusions. One, that this science as the principal one commands all the others; second,
40 that it uses for its own sake all other sciences which are its

vassals, as is evident in all ordered arts, where the end of one comes under the end of another. For example, pharmacy, which is the art of preparing remedies, is ordered to the end of medicine, which is health. Thus the physician orders the
5 pharmacist and uses the medicines made by him for his own end. So too, since the end of philosophy in its entirety is below the end of theology, and ordered to it, theology ought to order the other sciences and use what is taught in them.

Ad 1. It should be said that although philosophy treats of
10 existing things according to concepts derived from creatures, there must be another science which considers existing things according to notions received by the inspiration of the divine light.

Ad 2. From this the solution to the second objection is
15 clear. Philosophy suffices for the perfection of intellect by natural knowledge, and of the affections by means of acquired virtue. But there must be another science through which intellect is perfected in the order of infused knowledge, and the affections by gratuitous love.

20 *Ad* 3. It should be said that in those things which acquire an equal goodness for their end, the argument set forth, namely, this is more noble than that which cannot achieve its end by itself. But that which acquires perfect goodness by many aids and activities is more noble than that which acquires an
25 imperfect goodness through fewer means, or by itself, as the Philosopher says in *On the Heavens* 12. Thus is man, who is made to participate in divine glory itself, compared to other creatures.

30

Article 2
Should there be only one doctrine beyond the natural sciences?

35 *We proceed to the second question thus:*

1. It seems that there are several sciences and not just one beyond the natural sciences. Whatever a man can learn by concepts drawn from creatures, he can also learn by divine notions. But there are several sciences which employ creaturely
40 concepts, differing in kind and in species, such as moral,

natural, etc. Therefore sciences proceeding from divine notions ought to be many.

2. Again, each science is concerned with one kind of thing, as the Philosopher says in *Posterior Analytics* 1. But God and
5 creature, both treated in divine doctrine, cannot be reduced to one genus, neither univocally nor analogically. Therefore divine science is not one. Proof of the middle. Whatever agree in genus whether univocally or analogically, share something the same, whether according to prior and posterior—as substance
10 and accident share in the notion of being—or equally, as horse and cow share in the notion of animal. But God and creature do not share in anything that would be prior to and simpler than both. Therefore they are in no way reduced to one genus.

3. Again, the things we do, like acts of virtue, and the
15 things nature does, are not contained in the same science, for the one pertains to moral, the other to natural science. But divine science deals with the things we do, treating virtues and precepts, and it also deals with things which are not our works, like angels and other creatures. It seems, then, that it is not one
20 science.

ON THE CONTRARY: Whatever agree in one notion can belong to the same science. Hence all things, insofar as they come together in the notion of being, pertain to metaphysics. But divine science treats things under a divine formality which
25 embraces them all: all things are from him and for him. Therefore, although one, it can treat diverse things.

Moreover, things that belong to diverse sciences are treated in different books. But Sacred Scripture mixes everything, sometimes treating of morals, sometimes of the creator,
30 sometimes of creatures, as is evident in practically all its books. Therefore the science is not diversified on this basis.

SOLUTION: I reply that on this question it should be noted that knowledge is higher to the degree that it is more unified and extends to more things. Hence, God's intellect,
35 which is highest, has distinct knowledge of all things through something one, which is God himself. So too, since this science is highest and derives its efficacy from the light of divine inspiration itself and, while remaining one and undivided, considers diverse things, and not just universally, like
40 metaphysics, which considers all things insofar as they are

beings, without descending to proper knowledge of moral matters or of natural things. Since the notion of being is diversified in diverse things metaphysics is insufficient for specific knowledge of them. But the divine light, remaining one
5　in itself, is efficacious to make them manifest, as Dionysius says at the beginning of the *Celestial Hierarchy*.

Ad 1. The divine light, from the certitude of which this science proceeds, is efficacious in making manifest the many things which are treated in the different sciences of philosophy
10　which proceed from conceptions of these things to knowledge. Therefore there is no need for this science to be divided.

Ad 2. The creator and creature are reduced to one, not by a community of univocation, but of analogy. This is of two kinds. Either it arises from this that things share in something in
15　greater or lesser degrees, as potency and act—and substance and accident—share the notion of being. Or it arises from this that one thing receives its being and definition from another, and such is the analogy of creature to creator: the creature exists only to the degree that it descends from the primary
20　being, and it is called being only because it imitates the first being. Thus it is with wisdom and all the other things which are said of the creature.

Ad 3. The things we do and the things nature does, taken in their proper notions, do not fall to the same science. However,
25　one science having its certitude from the divine light, which is efficacious for knowledge of both, can consider both.

It might also be said that the virtues the theologian considers are not our work, but that God effects them in us without us, as Augustine says in *On Free Will*, 2.19.

COMMENTARY ON
BOETHIUS' *ON THE TRINITY*

QUESTION II
Concerning the Manifestation of Knowledge of Divine Truth

5

Article 1
Whether Divine Truths Ought to Be Treated of by the Method of Inquiry

10   *Objections*

1. It seems that it is not permissible to investigate divine things by the arguments of reason. In Sirach 3:22, it is said: "Seek not the things that are too high for thee"; but divine truths are, in a special way, too high for man, and particularly those truths which
15 are of faith; therefore it is not permissible to inquire into them.

2. Punishment is not inflicted except for some fault; but, as it is said in Prov. 25:27, "He that is a searcher of majesty shall be overwhelmed by glory"; therefore, it is not right to search out those things which pertain to divine majesty.

20   3. Ambrose says: "Abandon arguments where faith is sought." But in regard to divine truths, especially those concerned with the Trinity, faith is required; therefore in this matter it is not permissible to inquire into truth by arguments of reason.

4. Ambrose, in speaking of divine generation, says: "Supernal
25 mysteries are not to be scrutinized: one may know that the Son was begotten; but how He was begotten should not be analyzed." Accordingly, for the same reason it is not permissible to make rational investigation of those truths which pertain to the Trinity.

5. Gregory in his Homily for Easter (chap. 8) says: "Faith has
30 no merit where human reason affords proof"; but it is wrong to lose the merit of faith; therefore it is not right to investigate matters of faith according to methods of reason.

6. All honor ought to be given to God: but divine mysteries are honored by silence; wherefore Dionysius says at the close of Coel. hier.: "Honoring by silence the hidden truth which is above us"; and with this there agrees what is said in Psalm 64, according
5 to the text of Jerome: "Praise grows silent before You, O God," that is, silence itself is Your praise, O God; therefore we ought to refrain ourselves in silence from searching into divine truths.

7. No one is moved to infinity, as the Philosopher says in I *De Coelo et mundo*, because all motion is on account of the attaining of
10 an end [terminus], which is not to be found in infinity; but God is infinitely distant from us. Since, therefore, investigation is a kind of motion of reason toward that which is being searched out, it appears that divine truths ought not to be investigated.

15   *Sed contra*

On the other hand, it is said (1 Pet. 3:15): "Being ready always to satisfy everyone that asketh you a reason of that (faith and) hope which is in you"; but this could not be done unless we inquired reasonably into those things which are matters of faith;
20 therefore investigation according to methods of reason into the truths of faith is necessary.

Again as is said in Titus 1:9, it pertains to a bishop that he be capable of exhorting in sound doctrine and of overcoming those contradicting it: but he cannot do this without use of
25 argumentation; therefore one ought to employ the arguments of reason in matters of faith.

Again Augustine says in I *De Trinitate*: "With the help of God our Lord, we shall begin to discuss according to reason that for which they [our adversaries] seek explanation: that the Trinity is
30 one God." Therefore man can inquire about the Trinity according to methods of reason.

Also Augustine says in his argument against Felician: "Since without too much disagreement you recognize these two things— since you do not disregard the foregoing argument and the word
35 of authority—I present the matter to follow in such a way that you yourself may accept it as proof"; that is, I shall make use of arguments from reason and authority; and thus the conclusion is like the previous one.

Response. I answer that it must be said that, since the
40 perfection of man consists in his union with God, it is right that man, by all the means which are in his power and in so far as he is able, mount up to and strive to attain to divine truths, so that his

intellect may take delight in contemplation and his reason in the investigation of things of God, according to the saying of Ps. 72:28, "It is good for me to adhere to my God." Hence also the Philosopher in X *Ethic.* opposes the saying of those who
5 maintained that man ought not concern himself about divine things, but only about such as are human, saying: "One ought to be wise in regard to man, however, not according to those treating of human affairs alone, as a mortal knowing only mortal things; but, inasmuch as it is fitting for a mortal man to do so, he
10 ought to do all things according to the best of those powers that are in him."

In a threefold manner, however, it is possible for man to err on this point:

First, by presumption, since one might enter upon such
15 investigation as if he could attain a perfect comprehension, and it is this kind of presumption that is denounced in Job 11:7: "Do you think you can comprehend the steps of God, and find out the Almighty perfectly?" And Hilary says: "Do not involve yourself in the hiddenness and mystery of this inconceivable nativity; do not
20 overwhelm yourself, presuming to comprehend the loftiest of intelligible things, but understand that it is incomprehensible."

In the second place, error arises if, in matters of faith, reason has precedence of faith and not faith of reason, to the point that one would be willing to believe only what he could know by
25 reason, when the converse ought to be the case: wherefore Hilary says: "While believing [in a spirit of faith], inquire, discuss, carry through your speculation."

In a third way error results from undertaking an inquiry into divine things which are beyond one's capacity. Wherefore it is said
30 in Rom. 12:3, "Not to be more wise than it behoveth to be wise, but to be wise unto sobriety and according as God hath divided to every one the measure of faith." All men, indeed, have not been accorded the same measure; wherefore a thing is beyond the capacity of one which is not beyond that of another.
35

Answers to objections

1. It may be said: Those things are said to be too high for man which exceed his capacity, not those things which are of greater dignity according to nature: for the more man fixes his gaze upon
40 things loftier by nature, in accordance with his capacity, the more it is to his advantage; but in the consideration of things which in the least exceed his capacity, he easily falls into error. Therefore

the gloss on this same passage says: "Heretics are produced in two ways: namely, when men, beyond their proper capacity entering upon inquiry concerning the Creator or creatures fall into errors and depart from the truth."

5   2. Answer may be made: To search out is, as it were, to press one's investigation to the very end; but this would be unlawful and presumptuous if one should so investigate divine truths as though he could attain to complete comprehension as his goal.

3. It is answered: Where faith is sought for, those arguments
10 which are in opposition to faith and those which seek to have precedence over it are cast aside, but not those which in due manner follow it.

4. It may be said: It is not lawful in this world to inquire into divine mysteries in such a way that one would have the intention
15 of comprehending them, as is evident from the words that follow: "It is lawful to know that He was begotten," etc. For he undertakes an unlawful mode of inquiry who seeks to know what the nature of this nativity is, since in regard to divine things we are able to know what they are not, but not what they are.

20   5. It may be answered: Human reasoning may be spoken of in two ways: in one way, it may be regarded as demonstrative, forcing the intellect to believe; and this kind of reasoning cannot be possessed in regard to those truths which are of faith; but it is possible to possess this kind of reasoning in refuting those
25 arguments which would destroy faith or assert the impossible. For, although reason cannot demonstrate those things which are of faith, neither can these same truths be demonstratively disproved. Moreover, if this kind of reason could lead to a proving of those things which are of faith, it would deprive man of the merit of
30 faith, because then assent would not be voluntary, but necessary.

Persuasive reasoning, however, derived from certain likenesses to those things which are set forth by faith does not void the meaning of faith, since it does not make these truths to be apparent, for there can be no resolution of them to those first
35 principles discernable by the intellect. Nor does it take away the merit of faith, because it does not force the intellect to comprehend truth, but assent remains voluntary.

6. It may be said: God is honored by silence, but not in such a way that we may say nothing of Him or make no inquiries about
40 Him, but, inasmuch as we understand that we lack ability to comprehend Him. Wherefore in Sirach 43: 32-34, "Glorify the Lord as much as ever you can, for He will yet far exceed, and His

magnificence is wonderful. Blessing the Lord, exalt Him as much as you can: for He is above all praise. When you exalt Him put forth all your strength, and be not weary: for you can never go far enough."

5   7. Answer may be made: Since God is infinitely distant from creatures, no creature is so moved unto God as to be made His equal, either in receiving from Him or in knowing Him. Therefore, by reason of the fact that God is infinitely distant from creatures, there is no terminus to the motion of creatures; but

10   every creature is moved to this: that he may be more and more like to God, so far as this is possible, and so also the human mind ought always be moved more and more to a knowledge of God, according to the measure that is proper to it. Therefore Hilary says: "He who in pious spirit undertakes the infinite, even though

15   he can in no wise attain it, nevertheless profits by advancing."

Article 2
Whether There Can Be Any Science of Divine Truths Which Are Matters of Faith

20

Objections

1. it appears that there can be no science of those divine truths which are matters of faith. For wisdom is distinguished from science; but wisdom treats of divine truths; therefore science

25   cannot do so.

2. As is said in I *Poster.*, in every science one must suppose a quidditative knowledge of the subject; but in regard to God, it is impossible for us to know in any way what He is, as Damascene says; therefore it is not possible to possess any science of God.

30   3. It pertains to every science to consider the parts and passive potencies of its subject; but, since God is simple form [absolute act], He has not any parts that can be distinguished, nor in Him can there be any passive potencies; therefore there can be no science about God.

35   4. In any science, reason precedes assent, for it is demonstration which in the sciences makes one assent to what is knowable; but in regard to those truths which are of faith, the converse ought to prevail, namely, assent on account of faith ought to precede reason, as has been said; therefore, of divine

40   truths, especially of those which are known by faith, there can be no science.

5. Every science proceeds from self-evident principles which every man accepts upon first hearing, or from principles in which he has faith because of those first principles; but the articles of faith which are first principles in matters of faith, are not
5 principles of this same kind, since they are not *per se nota* nor can they be resolved by demonstration to those that are, as has been said; therefore, there can be no science of divine truths held by faith.

6. Faith is not of those things that are apparent: but science is
10 of things that are apparent, because through science those things that are treated of come to be clearly seen; therefore, concerning divine truths that are held by faith there can be no science.

7. Understanding is the principle of every science, because from the intellection of principles one comes to scientific
15 knowledge of conclusions: but in those things that are of faith, intellection is not the beginning, but the end, for, as is said in Is. 7:9, "If you will not believe, you shall not understand"; therefore there can be no science of divine truths held by faith.

20   **Sed contra**

But on the contrary is what Augustine says in XII *De Trinitate*: "To that science only do I attribute any value by which faith is well served, which leads to, produces, defends, and strengthens happiness"; therefore there is a science of the truths of faith.

25   Also, Wis. 10:10: "She gave him the science of the saints", that is, of the truths of faith, because no other science can be here meant except that by which saints are distinguished from sinners, which is the science of faith.

Also the Apostle in speaking of the knowledge of the faithful
30 says in 1 Cor. 8:7: "But there is not knowledge in everyone," and thus we come to the same conclusion as before.

Response. I answer that, since the essence of science consists in this, that from things known a knowledge of things previously unknown is derived, and this may occur in relation to divine
35 truths, evidently there can be a science of divine things.

But knowledge of divine truths can be thought of in two ways. In one way, as on our part, such truths are not knowable except from created things, of which we have a knowledge derived from sense experience. In another way, on the part of the nature of
40 these things themselves, they are, in themselves, most knowable; and although they are not known by us according to their essences, they are known by God and by the blessed according to their

proper mode; and so science of divine things must be considered in a twofold manner. One is according to our mode of knowledge, in which knowledge of sensible things serves as the principle for coming to a knowledge of divine; and it was in this way that the
5 philosophers handed down a traditional science of divine things, calling first philosophy a divine science. The other mode is according to that of divine things themselves as they are understood in themselves. This is, indeed, a mode of knowledge which we cannot possess perfectly in this life; but there is for us,
10 even in this life, a certain participation and assimilation to such a cognition of divine truth, inasmuch as through the faith which is infused into our souls we adhere to the very First Truth on account of Itself. And as God, since He knows Himself, knows in a way that is His own, that is, by simple intuition, not by discursive
15 thought, so we, from those truths that we possess in adhering to First Truth, come to a knowledge of other truths, according to our own mode of cognition, namely, by proceeding from principles to conclusions. Wherefore, those truths that we hold in the first place by faith are for us, as it were, first principles in this
20 science, and the other truths to which we attain are quasi-conclusions. From this it is evident that this science is of a higher order than that which the philosophers traditionally termed divine, since it proceeds from higher principles.

25 **Answers to objections**

1. It may be said: Wisdom is not distinguished from science as opposed to it, but as related to science by adding to it. For wisdom is, indeed, as the Philosopher says in VI *Ethic.*, the head of all the sciences, regulating all others inasmuch as it treats of
30 highest principles: on this account it is also called "the goddess of sciences" in I *Metaph.*; and much more is this true of that wisdom which is not only about highest principles, but from highest principles. Moreover, the function of wisdom is to order, and therefore this highest science, which orders and rules all others, is
35 called wisdom; just as in mechanical arts we call those men wise who direct others, as the architects: but the name of "science" is also left to others that are inferior, and accordingly science is distinguished from wisdom as a property from a definition (i.e., as properties flow necessarily from an essence, so do the other
40 sciences from wisdom).

2. It may be said: As has been previously declared, since causes are known through their effects, the knowledge of an effect

substitutes for the quidditative knowledge of the cause; this is
necessarily required in those sciences treating of things that cannot
be known through themselves: thus, for us to have a science of
divine things, it is not necessary that we first have a quidditative
5 knowledge of God. Or, again, it can be said that what we know
God is not, takes the place, in divine science, of a cognition of
what He is: for as one thing is distinguished from others by what it
is, so God is here known by that which He is not.

　　3. It may be answered: In science the parts of a subject are not
10 to be understood only as subjective or integral parts; but the parts
of a subject are all those things of which knowledge is required in
order to have cognition of the subject, since all things of this sort
are not dealt with in a co-science except inasmuch as they are
related to the subject. Those also are called passive potencies
15 which can be proved in regard to anything, whether they are
negations or relations to other things. And many such things can
be proved in regard to God, both from naturally known principles
and from principles of faith.

　　4. It may be answered: In any science whatever there are
20 certain things that serve as principles, and others as conclusions.
Hence the reasoning process set forth in the sciences precedes the
assent given to a conclusion, but follows upon assent to principles,
since it proceeds from them. Now, it is true that the articles of
faith are in this science rather principles than conclusions, but they
25 must be defended against those opposing them, as the Philosopher
(IV *Metaph.*) proves against those denying first principles: for they
may be made clearer of understanding by certain similitudes, by
inducing results of opposing naturally known principles, but they
cannot be proved by demonstrative reasoning.

30　　5. It must be said: Even in those sciences handed down to us
by human tradition, there are certain principles in some of them
which are not universally known, but which presuppose truths
derived from a higher science, just as in subordinate sciences
certain things taken from superior sciences are assumed and
35 believed to be true; and truths of this kind are not per se nota
except in the higher sciences. This is the case with the articles of
faith; for they are principles of that science leading to knowledge
of divine things, since those truths which are *per se nota* in the
knowledge which God has of Himself, are presupposed in our
40 science; and He is believed as the one manifesting these truths to
us through His messengers, even as the doctor believes from the
word of the physicist that there are four elements.

6. Answer is made: The evident truths of a science proceed from the evident truth of principles. Wherefore a science does not make clear the truth of its principles, but makes clear that of its conclusions: and in this same way the science of which we now
5   speak does not make evident the things of which we have faith, but on the basis of them, it makes other things evident with the same certitude as that belonging to their first principles.

7. It may be said: Understanding is always the first principle of any science, but not always the proximate principle; rather, it is
10   often faith which is the proximate principle of a science, as is evident in the case of the subordinate sciences; since their conclusions proceed from faith in truths accepted on the authority of a superior science as from a proximate principle, but from the understanding of scientists in the superior field who have
15   intellectual certitude of these created truths as from their ultimate principle. So likewise the proximate principle of this divine science is faith, but the first principle is the divine intellect to the revelation of which we give the assent of faith; but faith is in us that we may attain to an understanding of those things we believe;
20   in the same way that a scientist in an inferior field, if he should gain knowledge of a higher, would then possess understanding and science of truths which previously were accepted only on faith.

25
Article 3
Whether in the Science of Faith, Which Is Concerning God, it Is Permissible to Use the Rational Arguments of the Natural Philosophers

30   *Objections*

1. It seems that in regard to those truths that are of faith it is not right to employ the rational arguments of the natural philosophers, for, according to 1 Cor. 1:17, "Christ sent me not to baptize, but to preach the gospel: not kisdom of speech"; that
35   is, "in the doctrine of the philosophers," as the gloss says. And concerning the line (1 Cor. 1:20), "Where is the disputer of this world?" the gloss says: "The disputer is he who searches into the secrets of nature; such men God does not accept as preachers." And on the line (1 Cor. 2:4), "And my speech and my preaching
40   was not in the persuasive words of human wisdom," the gloss says: "Although the words were persuasive, they were not so because of human wisdom, as is the word of pseudo-apostlcs."

From all these lines it is evident that in matters of faith it is not lawful to employ philosophical reasoning.

2. On that line (Is. 15:1), "Because in the night Ar of Moab is laid waste," the gloss says: "Ar, that is, the adversary, namely, 5 secular science, which is the adversary of God"; therefore, etc.

3. Ambrose says: "The deepest mysteries of faith are free from the reasonings of the philosophers"; therefore, when a matter of faith is dealt with, the reasonings and words of the philosophers ought not to be used.

10   4. Jerome relates in a letter to Eustochium that in vision he was beaten, according to divine justice, because he had read the books of Cicero, and that those standing by besought that leniency might be granted on account of his youth, and that afterward the extreme penalty should be exacted if he read again the books of 15 the Gentiles; wherefore, calling upon the name of God, he exclaimed: "If ever I shall possess secular books, if ever I read them, I shall have denied You"; therefore it is not lawful to use them in treating of divine things.

5. In Scripture, secular wisdom is often represented by water, 20 but divine wisdom by wine. Now, according to Is., chap. 1, the innkeepers are upbraided for mixing water with wine; therefore the doctors are blameworthy for their mingling of philosophical doctrine with sacred Scripture.

6. Jerome says, in his gloss on Hosea, chap. 2, "With heretics 25 we ought not to have even names in common." But heretics use the arguments of philosophers to destroy faith, as is maintained in the gloss on Prov., chap, 7 and Is., chap. 15; therefore Catholics ought not to use such in their discussions.

7. Every science has its proper principles, and thus also sacred 30 doctrine has those that belong to it, namely, the articles of faith; but in other sciences the process is not valid if principles are saken from a different science, but each ought to proceed from its own principles, according to the teaching of the Philosopher (I *Poster.*); therefore the method is not permissible in sacred doctrine.

35   8. If the doctrine of anyone is repudiated in any respect, the authority of his teaching will not be valid in proving anything; wherefore Augustine says that, if in sacred doctrine we discover some falsity, the authority of that teaching is destroyed for confirming anything in regard to faith; but sacred doctrine 40 repudiates the doctrine of the philosophers in many ways, because many errors are found among them; therefore their authority has no efficacy in proving anything (regarding sacred doctrine).

Sed contra

But on the contrary, the Apostle (Titus 1: 12) makes use of a verse from the poet Epimenides, saying, "The Cretans are always
5 liars, evil beasts," etc.; and (1 Cor. 15:33) he employs the words of Menander: "Evil communications corrupt good manners"; and in Acts 17:28 are the words of Aratus, "For we are also his (i.e., God's) offspring." Therefore it is licit for other doctors of divine Scripture also to make use of the arguments of the philosophers.

10 Again, Jerome, in a letter to Magnus, a famous orator of Rome, having enumerated many doctors of Scripture, such as Basil and Gregory, adds: "All these have so intermingled in their books the teachings and the sayings of the philosophers that one knows not which to admire first in them, their secular erudition or their
15 knowledge of the Scriptures." But this they would not have done had such been illicit or useless.

Also Jerome in a letter to Pammachius about the death of Paula says: you have become enamored of the captive woman, secular wisdom, and captivated by her beauty, cut her hair and her
20 finger nails, cut away the enticement of her tresses and the adornments of her words, bathe her with prophetic niter, and, lying with her, say: 'His left hand under my head, and his right hand shall embrace me' (Cant. 8:3), and many children will the captive woman give to you, and from the Moabite, Israelites will
25 be born to you." Therefore with fruitful results some make use of secular wisdom.

Again Augustine (II *De Trinitate*) says: "I shall not be without zeal in seeking out knowledge of God, whether through Scripture or creatures"; but knowledge of God through creaturegis given in
30 philosophy; therefore it is not unfitting that in sacred doctrine one should make use of philosophical reasoning.

Again Augustine (Book II, *De doctrina Christiana*) says: "If the philosophers have by chance uttered truths helpful to our faith, they are not only not to be feared, but rather those truths ought to
35 be taken from them as from unjust possessors and used to our advantage." Thus the conclusion is as before.

Also on the saying in Dan. 1:8, "But Daniel purposed in his heart," the gloss says: "If anyone ignorant of mathematics should write in opposition to the mathematicians, or knowing nothing of
40 philosophy should argue against the philosophers, would he not be derided?" But doctors of sacred Scripture must at times argue with

philosophers; therefore it is needful that they make use of philosophy.

Response. I answer that it must be said that gifts of grace are
5 added to those of nature in such a way that they do not destroy the latter, but rather perfect them; wherefore also the light of faith, which is gratuitously infused into our minds, does not destroy the natural light of cognition, which is in us by natuise. For although the natural light of the human mind is insufficient to reveal those
10 truths revealed by faith, yet it is impossible that those things which God has manifested to us by faith should be contrary to those which are evident to us by natural knowledge. In this case one would necessarily be false: and since both kinds of truth are from God, God would be the author of error, a thing which is
15 impossible. Rather, since in imperfect things there is found some imitation of the perfect, though the image is deficient, in those things known by natural reason there are certain similitudes of the truths revealed by faith. Now, as sacred doctrine is founded upon the light of faith, so philosophy depends upon the light of natural
20 reason; wherefore it is impossible that philosophical truths are contrary to those that are of faith; but they are deficient as compared to them. Nevertheless they incorporate some similitudes of those higher truths, and some things that are preparatory for them, just as nature is the preamble to grace.
25 If, however, anything is found in the teachings of the philosophers contrary to faith, this error does not properly belong to philosophy, but is due to an abuse of philosophy owing to the insufficiency of reason. Therefore also it is possible from the principles of philosophy to refute an error of this kind, either by
30 showing it to be altogether impossible, or not to be necessary. For just as those things which are of faith cannot be demonstratively proved, so certain things contrary to them cannot be demonstratively shown to be false, but they can be shown not to be necessary.
35 Thus, in sacred doctrine we are able to make a threefold use of philosophy:

1. First, to demonstrate those truths that are preambles of faith and that have a necessary place in the science of faith. Such are the truths about God that can be proved by natural reason—
40 that God exists, that God is one; such truths about God or about His creatures, subject to philosophical proof, faith presupposes.

2. Secondly, to give a clearer notion, by certain similitudes, of the truths of faith, as Augustine in his book, *De Trinitate*, employed any comparisons taken from the teachings of the philosophers to aid understanding of the Trinity.

5 3. In the third place, to resist those who speak against the faith, either by showing that their statements are false, or by showing that they are not necessarily true.

Nevertheless, in the use of philosophy in sacred Scripture, there can be a twofold error:

10 In one way, by using doctrines contrary to faith, which are not truths of philosophy, but rather error, or abuse of philosophy, as Origen did.

In another way, by using them in such manner as to include under the measure of philosophy truths of faith, as if one should be 15 willing to believe nothing except what could be held by philosophic reasoning; when, on the contrary, philosophy should be subject to the measure of faith, according to the saying of the Apostle (2 Cor. 10:5), "Bringing into captivity every understanding unto the obedience of Christ."

20

Answers to objections

1. It may be said: From all these words it is shown that philosophical doctrine ought not to be used as if it had first place, as if on account of it one believed by faith; nevertheless the fact is 25 not disproved that doctors of sacred learning may employ philosophy, as it were, secondarily. Wherefore, on the saying (1 Cor. 1:19), "I will destroy the wisdom of the wise," the gloss adds: "This he does not say because the understanding of truth can be worthy of God's anger, but because the false prudence of those 30 who trusted in their erudition is worthy of reproof."

Nevertheless, in order that all that is of faith might be attributed not to human power or wisdom but to God, God willed that the primitive preaching of the apostles should be in infirmity and simplicity; though, on the other hand, with the later advent of 35 power and secular wisdom, He manifested by the victory of the faith that the world is subject to God as much by wisdom as by power.

2. It may be said: Secular wisdom is said to be contrary to God in so far as it is an abuse of wisdom (i.e., erroneous) as when 40 heretics abuse it, but not in so far as it is true.

3. It may be answered: The sacred deposit of the truth of faith is said to be free from philosophical doctrine inasmuch as it is not confined by the limits of philosophy.

4. It may be said: Jerome was so influenced by certain books
5 of the Gentiles that he contemned, in a way, sacred Scripture: wherefore he himself says: "If I began to read it while turning over the words of the Prophets in my own mind, their crude expression filled me with distaste." And no one will deny that such was reprehensible.

10   5. It may be said: No conclusive argument can be drawn from figurative speech, as the Master (Peter Lombard) says. Dionysius also says in his letter to Titus that symbolic theology has no weight of proof, especially when such interprets no authority. Nevertheless it can be said that when one of two things passes into
15 the nature of another, the product is not considered a mixture except when the nature of both is altered. Wherefore those who use philosophical doctrines in sacred Scripture in such a way as to subject them to the service of faith, do not mix water with wine, but change water into wine.

20   6. It may be said: Jerome is speaking of those arguments that were invented by heretics to give support to their errors; but such doctrines do not belong to philosophy; rather they lead only to error; and consequently on their account the truths of philosophy ought not be shunned.

25   7. Answer may be made: Sciences which are ordered to one another are so related that one can use the principles of another, just as posterior sciences can use the principles of prior sciences, whether they are superior or inferior: wherefore metaphysics, which is superior in dignity to all, uses truths that have been
30 proved in other sciences. And in like manner theology—although all other sciences are related to it in the order of generation, as serving it and as preambles to it—can make use of the principles of all the others, even if they are posterior to it in dignity.

8. It may be said: Inasmuch as sacred doctrine makes use of
35 the teachings of philosophy for their own sake, it does not accept them on account of the authority of those who taught them, but on account of the reasonableness of the doctrine; wherefore it accepts truth well said and rejects other things: but when it uses these doctrines to refute certain errors, it uses them inasmuch as
40 their authority is esteemed by those whose refutation is desired, because the testimony of an adversary has in that case greater weight.

SUMMA CONTRA GENTILES

FIRST BOOK
[On God]

CHAPTER I

IN WHAT CONSISTS THE OFFICE OF A WISE MAN

My mouth shall meditate truth, and my lips shall hate wickedness.
—PROV. viii. 7.

THE general use which, in the Philosopher's opinion, should be
followed in naming things, has resulted in those men being called
wise who direct things themselves and govern them well.
Wherefore among other things which men conceive of the wise
5 man, the Philosopher reckons that it belongs to the wise man to
direct things. Now the rule of all things directed to the end of
government and order must needs be taken from their end: for
then is a thing best disposed when it is fittingly directed to its end,
since the end of everything is its good. Wherefore in the arts we
10 observe that the art which governs and rules another is the one to
which the latter's end belongs: thus the medical art rules and
directs the art of the druggist, because health which is the object of
medicine is the end of all drugs which are made up by the
druggist's art. The same may be observed in the art of sailing in
15 relation to the art of ship-building, and in the military art in
relation to the equestrian art and all warlike appliances. These arts
which govern others are called master-arts (*architectonicæ*), that is
principal arts, for which reason their craftsmen, who are called
master-craftsmen (*architectores*), are awarded the name of wise
20 men. Since, however, these same craftsmen, through being
occupied with the ends of certain singular things, do not attain to
the universal end of all things, they are called wise about this or

that, in which sense it is said (1 Cor. iii. 10): As a wise architect, I have laid the foundation; whereas the name of being wise simply is reserved to him alone whose consideration is about the end of the universe, which end is also the beginning of the universe:
5 wherefore, according to the Philosopher, it belongs to the wise man to consider the highest causes.

Now the last end of each thing is that which is intended by the first author or mover of that thing: and the first author and mover of the universe is an intellect, as we shall prove further on.
10 Consequently the last end of the universe must be the good of the intellect: and this is truth. Therefore truth must be the last end of the whole universe; and the consideration thereof must be the chief occupation of wisdom. And for this reason divine Wisdom, clothed in flesh, declares that He came into the world to make
15 known the truth, saying (Jo. xviii. 37): For this was I born, and for this cause came I into the world, that I should give testimony to the truth. Moreover the Philosopher defines the First Philosophy as being the knowledge of truth, not of any truth, but of that truth which is the source of all truth, of that, namely, which relates to
20 the first principle of being of all things; wherefore its truth is the principle of all truth, since the disposition of things is the same in truth as in being.

Now it belongs to the same thing to pursue one contrary and to remove the other: thus medicine which effects health, removes
25 sickness. Hence, just as it belongs to a wise man to meditate and disseminate truth, especially about the first principle, so does it belong to him to refute contrary falsehood.

Wherefore the twofold office of the wise man is fittingly declared from the mouth of Wisdom, in the words above quoted;
30 namely, to meditate and publish the divine truth, which antonomastically is the truth, as signified by the words, My mouth shall meditate truth; and to refute the error contrary to truth, as signified by the words, and my lips shall hate wickedness, by which is denoted falsehood opposed to divine truth, which
35 falsehood is contrary to religion that is also called godliness, wherefore the falsehood that is contrary thereto receives the name of ungodliness.

CHAPTER II

THE AUTHOR'S INTENTION IN THIS WORK

5   Now of all human pursuits, that of wisdom is the most perfect, the most sublime, the most profitable, the most delightful. It is the most perfect, since in proportion as a man devotes himself to the pursuit of wisdom, so much does he already share in true happiness: wherefore the wise man says (Ecclus. xiv.
10 22): Blessed is the man that shall continue in wisdom. It is the most sublime because thereby especially does man approach to a likeness to God, Who made all things in wisdom: wherefore since likeness is the cause of love, the pursuit of wisdom especially unites man to God by friendship: hence it is said (Wis. vii. 14) that
15 wisdom is an infinite treasure to men: which they that use, become the friends of God. It is the most profitable, because by wisdom itself man is brought to the kingdom of immortality, for the desire of wisdom bringeth to the everlasting kingdom (Wis. vi. 21). And it is the most delightful because her conversation hath no
20 bitterness, nor her company any tediousness, but joy and gladness (Wis. viii. 16).

    Wherefore, taking heart from God's lovingkindness to assume the office of a wise man, although it surpasses our own powers, the purpose we have in view is, in our own weak way, to declare
25 the truth which the Catholic faith professes, while weeding out contrary errors; for, in the words of Hilary, I acknowledge that I owe my life's chief occupation to God, so that every word and every thought of mine may speak of Him. But it is difficult to refute the errors of each individual, for two reasons. First, because
30 the sacrilegious assertions of each erring individual are not so well known to us, that we are able from what they say to find arguments to refute their errors. For the Doctors of old used this method in order to confute the errors of the heathens, whose opinions they were able to know, since either they had been
35 heathens themselves, or had lived among heathens and were conversant with their teachings. Secondly, because some of them, like the Mohammedans and pagans, do not agree with us as to the authority of any Scripture whereby they may be convinced, in the same way as we are able to dispute with the Jews by means of the
40 Old Testament, and with heretics by means of the New: whereas the former accept neither. Wherefore it is necessary to have

recourse to natural reason, to which all are compelled to assent. And yet this is deficient in the things of God.

And while we are occupied in the inquiry about a particular truth, we shall show what errors are excluded thereby, and how 5 demonstrable truth is in agreement with the faith of the Christian religion.

CHAPTER III

10

IN WHAT WAY IT IS POSSIBLE TO MAKE KNOWN THE DIVINE TRUTH

SINCE, however, not every truth is to be made known in the 15 same way, and it is the part of an educated man to seek for conviction in each subject, only so far as the nature of the subject allows, as the Philosopher most rightly observes as quoted by Boethius, it is necessary to show first of all in what way it is possible to make known the aforesaid truth.

20 Now in those things which we hold about God there is truth in two ways. For certain things that are true about God wholly surpass the capability of human reason, for instance that God is three and one: while there are certain things to which even natural reason can attain, for instance that God is, that God is one, and 25 others like these, which even the philosophers proved demonstratively of God, being guided by the light of natural reason.

That certain divine truths wholly surpass the capability of human reason, is most clearly evident. For since the principle of 30 all the knowledge which the reason acquires about a thing, is the understanding of that thing's essence, because according to the Philosopher's teaching the principle of a demonstration is what a thing is, it follows that our knowledge about a thing will be in proportion to our understanding of its essence. Wherefore, if the 35 human intellect comprehends the essence of a particular thing, for instance a stone or a triangle, no truth about that thing will surpass the capability of human reason. But this does not happen to us in relation to God, because the human intellect is incapable by its natural power of attaining to the comprehension of His essence: 40 since our intellect's knowledge, according to the mode of the present life, originates from the senses: so that things which are not objects of sense cannot be comprehended by the human

intellect, except in so far as knowledge of them is gathered from sensibles. Now sensibles cannot lead our intellect to see in them what God is, because they are effects unequal to the power of their cause. And yet our intellect is led by sensibles to the divine
5 knowledge so as to know about God that He is, and other such truths, which need to be ascribed to the first principle. Accordingly some divine truths are attainable by human reason, while others altogether surpass the power of human reason.

Again. The same is easy to see from the degrees of intellects.
10 For if one of two men perceives a thing with his intellect with greater subtlety, the one whose intellect is of a higher degree understands many things which the other is altogether unable to grasp; as instanced in a yokel who is utterly incapable of grasping the subtleties of philosophy. Now the angelic intellect surpasses
15 the human intellect more than the intellect of the cleverest philosopher surpasses that of the most uncultured. For an angel knows God through a more excellent effect than does man, for as much as the angel's essence, through which he is led to know God by natural knowledge, is more excellent than sensible things, even
20 than the soul itself, by which the human intellect mounts to the knowledge of God. And the divine intellect surpasses the angelic intellect much more than the angelic surpasses the human. For the divine intellect by its capacity equals the divine essence, wherefore God perfectly understands of Himself what He is, and He knows
25 all things that can be understood about Him: whereas the angel knows not what God is by his natural knowledge, because the angel's essence, by which he is led to the knowledge of God, is an effect unequal to the power of its cause. Consequently an angel is unable by his natural knowledge to grasp all that God understands
30 about Himself: nor again is human reason capable of grasping all that an angel understands by his natural power. Accordingly just as a man would show himself to be a most insane fool if he declared the assertions of a philosopher to be false because he was unable to understand them, so, and much more, a man would be
35 exceedingly foolish, were he to suspect of falsehood the things revealed by God through the ministry of His angels, because they cannot be the object of reason's investigations.

Furthermore. The same is made abundantly clear by the deficiency which every day we experience in our knowledge of
40 things. For we are ignorant of many of the properties of sensible things, and in many cases we are unable to discover the nature of those properties which we perceive by our senses. Much less

therefore is human reason capable of investigating all the truths about that most sublime essence.

With this the saying of the Philosopher is in accord (2 *Metaph.*) where he says that our intellect in relation to those
5 primary things which are most evident in nature is like the eye of a bat in relation to the sun.

To this truth Holy Writ also bears witness. For it is written (Job xi. 7): Peradventure thou wilt comprehend the steps of God and wilt find out the Almighty perfectly? and (xxxvi. 26): Behold
10 God is great, exceeding our knowledge, and (1 Cor. xiii. 9): We know in part.

Therefore all that is said about God, though it cannot be investigated by reason, must not be forthwith rejected as false, as the Manicheans and many unbelievers have thought.
15

CHAPTER IV

THAT THE TRUTH ABOUT DIVINE THINGS
20 WHICH IS ATTAINABLE BY REASON
IS FITTINGLY PROPOSED TO MAN AS AN OBJECT OF BELIEF

WHILE then the truth of the intelligible things of God is twofold, one to which the inquiry of reason can attain, the other
25 which surpasses the whole range of human reason, both are fittingly proposed by God to man as an object of belief. We must first show this with regard to that truth which is attainable by the inquiry of reason, lest it appears to some, that since it can be attained by reason, it was useless to make it an object of faith by
30 supernatural inspiration. Now three disadvantages would result if this truth were left solely to the inquiry of reason. One is that few men would have knowledge of God: because very many are hindered from gathering the fruit of diligent inquiry, which is the discovery of truth, for three reasons. Some indeed on account of
35 an indisposition of temperament, by reason of which many are naturally indisposed to knowledge: so that no efforts of theirs would enable them to reach to the attainment of the highest degree of human knowledge, which consists in knowing God. Some are hindered by the needs of household affairs. For there
40 must needs be among men some that devote themselves to the conduct of temporal affairs, who would be unable to devote so much time to the leisure of contemplative research as to reach the

summit of human inquiry, namely the knowledge of God. And some are hindered by laziness. For in order to acquire the knowledge of God in those things which reason is able to investigate, it is necessary to have a previous knowledge of many
5   things: since almost the entire consideration of philosophy is directed to the knowledge of God: for which reason metaphysics, which is about divine things, is the last of the parts of philosophy to be studied. Wherefore it is not possible to arrive at the inquiry about the aforesaid truth except after a most laborious study: and
10   few are willing to take upon themselves this labour for the love of a knowledge, the natural desire for which has nevertheless been instilled into the mind of man by God.

The second disadvantage is that those who would arrive at the discovery of the aforesaid truth would scarcely succeed in doing so
15   after a long time. First, because this truth is so profound, that it is only after long practice that the human intellect is enabled to grasp it by means of reason. Secondly, because many things are required beforehand, as stated above. Thirdly, because at the time of youth, the mind, when tossed about by the various movements of the
20   passions, is not fit for the knowledge of so sublime a truth, whereas calm gives prudence and knowledge, as stated in 7 *Phys*. Hence mankind would remain in the deepest darkness of ignorance, if the path of reason were the only available way to the knowledge of God: because the knowledge of God which
25   especially makes men perfect and good, would be acquired only by the few, and by these only after a long time.

The third disadvantage is that much falsehood is mingled with the investigations of human reason, on account of the weakness of our intellect in forming its judgments, and by reason of the
30   admixture of phantasms. Consequently many would remain in doubt about those things even which are most truly demonstrated, through ignoring the force of the demonstration: especially when they perceive that different things are taught by the various men who are called wise. Moreover among the many demonstrated
35   truths, there is sometimes a mixture of falsehood that is not demonstrated, but assumed for some probable or sophistical reason which at times is mistaken for a demonstration. Therefore it was necessary that definite certainty and pure truth about divine things should be offered to man by the way of faith.
40   Accordingly the divine clemency has made this salutary commandment, that even some things which reason is able to

investigate must be held by faith: so that all may share in the knowledge of God easily, and without doubt or error.

Hence it is written (Eph. iv. 17, 18): *That henceforward you walk not as also the Gentiles walk in the vanity of their mind, having their understanding darkened:* and (Isa. liv. 13): *All thy children shall be taught of the Lord.*

CHAPTER V

THAT THOSE THINGS WHICH CANNOT BE INVESTIGATED BY REASON ARE FITTINGLY PROPOSED TO MAN AS AN OBJECT OF FAITH

IT may appear to some that those things which cannot be investigated by reason ought not to be proposed to man as an object of faith: because divine wisdom provides for each thing according to the mode of its nature. We must therefore prove that it is necessary also for those things which surpass reason to be proposed by God to man as an object of faith.

For no man tends to do a thing by his desire and endeavour unless it be previously known to him. Wherefore since man is directed by divine providence to a higher good than human frailty can attain in the present life, as we shall show in the sequel, it was necessary for his mind to be bidden to something higher than those things to which our reason can reach in the present life, so that he might learn to aspire, and by his endeavours to tend to something surpassing the whole state of the present life. And this is especially competent to the Christian religion, which alone promises goods spiritual and eternal: for which reason it proposes many things surpassing the thought of man: whereas the old law which contained promises of temporal things, proposed few things that are above human inquiry. It was with this motive that the philosophers, in order to wean men from sensible pleasures to virtue, took care to show that there are other goods of greater account than those which appeal to the senses, the taste of which things affords much greater delight to those who devote themselves to active or contemplative virtues.

Again it is necessary for this truth to be proposed to man as an object of faith in order that he may have truer knowledge of God. For then alone do we know God truly, when we believe that He is far above all that man can possibly think of God, because the divine essence surpasses man's natural knowledge, as stated above. Hence by the fact that certain things about God are proposed to man, which surpass his reason, he is strengthened in his opinion that God is far above what he is able to think.

5   There results also another advantage from this, namely, the checking of presumption which is the mother of error. For some there are who presume so far on their wits that they think themselves capable of measuring the whole nature of things by their intellect, in that they esteem all things true which they see,

10   and false which they see not. Accordingly, in order that man's mind might be freed from this presumption, and seek the truth humbly, it was necessary that certain things far surpassing his intellect should be proposed to man by God.

Yet another advantage is made apparent by the words of the

15   Philosopher (10 *Ethic.*). For when a certain Simonides maintained that man should neglect the knowledge of God, and apply his mind to human affairs, and declared that a man ought to relish human things, and a mortal, mortal things: the Philosopher contradicted him, saying that a man ought to devote himself to immortal and

20   divine things as much as he can. Hence he says (II *De Anima*) that though it is but little that we perceive of higher substances, yet that little is more loved and desired than all the knowledge we have of lower substances. He says also (2 *De Coelo et Mundo*) that when questions about the heavenly bodies can be answered by a

25   short and probable solution, it happens that the hearer is very much rejoiced. All this shows that however imperfect the knowledge of the highest things may be, it bestows very great perfection on the soul: and consequently, although human reason is unable to grasp fully things that are above reason, it nevertheless

30   acquires much perfection, if at least it hold things, in any way whatever, by faith.

Wherefore it is written (Ecclus. iii. 25): Many things are shown to thee above the understanding of men, and (1 Cor. ii. 10, 11): The things . . . that are of God no man knoweth, but the

35   Spirit of God: but to us God hath revealed them by His Spirit.

CHAPTER VI

THAT IT IS NOT A MARK OF LEVITY TO ASSENT TO THE THINGS
THAT ARE OF FAITH, ALTHOUGH THEY ARE ABOVE REASON

5

Now those who believe this truth, of which reason affords a
proof, believe not lightly, as though following foolish fables (2
Pet. i. 16). For divine Wisdom Himself, Who knows all things
most fully, deigned to reveal to man the secrets of God's wisdom:
10 and by suitable arguments proves His presence, and the truth of
His doctrine and inspiration, by performing works surpassing the
capability of the whole of nature, namely, the wondrous healing of
the sick, the raising of the dead to life, a marvellous control over
the heavenly bodies, and what excites yet more wonder, the
15 inspiration of human minds, so that unlettered and simple persons
are filled with the Holy Ghost, and in one instant are endowed
with the most sublime wisdom and eloquence. And after
considering these arguments, convinced by the strength of the
proof, and not by the force of arms, nor by the promise of
20 delights, but—and this is the greatest marvel of all—amidst the
tyranny of persecutions, a countless crowd of not only simple but
also of the wisest men, embraced the Christian faith, which
inculcates things surpassing all human understanding, curbs the
pleasures of the flesh, and teaches contempt of all worldly things.
25 That the minds of mortal beings should assent to such things, is
both the greatest of miracles, and the evident work of divine
inspiration, seeing that they despise visible things and desire only
those that are invisible. And that this happened not suddenly nor
by chance, but by the disposition of God, is shown by the fact that
30 God foretold that He would do so by the manifold oracles of the
prophets, whose books we hold in veneration as bearing witness to
our faith. This particular kind of proof is alluded to in the words of
Heb. ii. 3, 4: Which, namely the salvation of mankind, having
begun to be declared by the Lord, was confirmed with us by them
35 that heard Him, God also bearing witness by signs and wonders,
and divers . . . distributions of the Holy Ghost.

Now such a wondrous conversion of the world to the
Christian faith is a most indubitable proof that such signs did take
place, so that there is no need to repeat them, seeing that there is
40 evidence of them in their result. For it would be the most
wondrous sign of all if without any wondrous signs the world were
persuaded by simple and lowly men to believe things so arduous,

to accomplish things so difficult, and to hope for things so sublime. Although God ceases not even in our time to work miracles through His saints in confirmation of the faith.

On the other hand those who introduced the errors of the
5   sects proceeded in contrary fashion, as instanced by Mohammed, who enticed peoples with the promise of carnal pleasures, to the desire of which the concupiscence of the flesh instigates. He also delivered commandments in keeping with his promises, by giving the reins to carnal pleasure, wherein it is easy for carnal men to
10   obey: and the lessons of truth which he inculcated were only such as can be easily known to any man of average wisdom by his natural powers: yea rather the truths which he taught were mingled by him with many fables and most false doctrines. Nor did he add any signs of supernatural agency, which alone are a
15   fitting witness to divine inspiration, since a visible work that can be from God alone, proves the teacher of truth to be invisibly inspired: but he asserted that he was sent in the power of arms, a sign that is not lacking even to robbers and tyrants. Again, those who believed in him from the outset were not wise men practised
20   in things divine and human, but beastlike men who dwelt in the wilds, utterly ignorant of all divine teaching; and it was by a multitude of such men and the force of arms that he compelled others to submit to his law.

Lastly, no divine oracles of prophets in a previous age bore
25   witness to him; rather did he corrupt almost all the teaching of the Old and New Testaments by a narrative replete with fables, as one may see by a perusal of his law. Hence by a cunning device, he did not commit the reading of the Old and New Testament Books to his followers, lest he should thereby be convicted of falsehood.
30   Thus it is evident that those who believe his words believe lightly.

CHAPTER VII

35   THAT THE TRUTH OF REASON IS NOT IN OPPOSITION TO THE
TRUTH OF THE CHRISTIAN FAITH

Now though the aforesaid truth of the Christian faith surpasses the ability of human reason, nevertheless those things which are
40   naturally instilled in human reason cannot be opposed to this truth. For it is clear that those things which are implanted in reason by nature, are most true, so much so that it is impossible to

think them to be false. Nor is it lawful to deem false that which is held by faith, since it is so evidently confirmed by God. Seeing then that the false alone is opposed to the true, as evidently appears if we examine their definitions, it is impossible for the
5 aforesaid truth of faith to be contrary to those principles which reason knows naturally.

Again. The same thing which the disciple's mind receives from its teacher is contained in the knowledge of the teacher, unless he teach insincerely, which it were wicked to say of God.
10 Now the knowledge of naturally known principles is instilled into us by God, since God Himself is the author of our nature. Therefore the divine Wisdom also contains these principles. Consequently whatever is contrary to these principles, is contrary to the divine Wisdom; wherefore it cannot be from God.
15 Therefore those things which are received by faith from divine revelation cannot be contrary to our natural knowledge.

Moreover. Our intellect is stayed by contrary arguments, so that it cannot advance to the knowledge of truth. Wherefore if conflicting knowledges were instilled into us by God, our intellect
20 would thereby be hindered from knowing the truth. And this cannot be ascribed to God.

Furthermore. Things that are natural are unchangeable so long as nature remains. Now contrary opinions cannot be together in the same subject. Therefore God does not instil into man any
25 opinion or belief contrary to natural knowledge.

Hence the Apostle says (Rom. x. 8): The word is nigh thee even in thy heart and in thy mouth. This is the word of faith which we preach. Yet because it surpasses reason some look upon it as though it were contrary thereto; which is impossible.
30 This is confirmed also by the authority of Augustine who says (*Gen. ad lit.* ii): That which truth shall make known can nowise be in opposition to the holy books whether of the Old or of the New Testament.

From this we may evidently conclude that whatever
35 arguments are alleged against the teachings of faith, they do not rightly proceed from the first self-evident principles instilled by nature. Wherefore they lack the force of demonstration, and are either probable or sophistical arguments, and consequently it is possible to solve them.
40

CHAPTER VIII

IN WHAT RELATION HUMAN REASON STANDS
TO THE TRUTH OF FAITH

5

IT would also seem well to observe that sensible things from which human reason derives the source of its knowledge, retain a certain trace of likeness to God, but so imperfect that it proves altogether inadequate to manifest the substance itself of God. For 10 effects resemble their causes according to their own mode, since like action proceeds from like agent; and yet the effect does not always reach to a perfect likeness to the agent. Accordingly human reason is adapted to the knowledge of the truth of faith, which can be known in the highest degree only by those who see the divine 15 substance, in so far as it is able to put together certain probable arguments in support thereof, which nevertheless are insufficient to enable us to understand the aforesaid truth as though it were demonstrated to us or understood by us in itself. And yet however weak these arguments may be, it is useful for the human mind to 20 be practised therein, so long as it does not pride itself on having comprehended or demonstrated: since although our view of the sublimest things is limited and weak, it is most pleasant to be able to catch but a glimpse of them, as appears from what has been said.

25   The authority of Hilary is in agreement with this statement: for he says (*De Trin.*) while speaking of this same truth: Begin by believing these things, advance and persevere; and though I know thou wilt not arrive, I shall rejoice at thy advance. For he who devoutly follows in pursuit of the infinite, though he never come 30 up with it, will always advance by setting forth. Yet pry not into that secret, and meddle not in the mystery of the birth of the infinite, nor presume to grasp that which is the summit of understanding: but understand that there are things thou canst not grasp.

35

CHAPTER IX

OF THE ORDER AND MODE OF PROCEDURE IN THIS WORK

40

ACCORDINGLY, from what we have been saying it is evident that the intention of the wise man must be directed to the twofold truth of divine things and to the refutation of contrary errors: and that the research of reason is able to reach to one of these, while the other surpasses every effort of reason. And I speak of a twofold truth of divine things, not on the part of God Himself

5 Who is Truth one and simple, but on the part of our knowledge, the relation of which to the knowledge of divine things varies.

Wherefore in order to deduce the first kind of truth we must proceed by demonstrative arguments whereby we can convince our adversaries. But since such arguments are not available in

10 support of the second kind of truth, our intention must be not to convince our opponent by our arguments, but to solve the arguments which he brings against the truth, because, as shown above, natural reason cannot be opposed to the truth of faith. In a special way may the opponent of this kind of truth be convinced

15 by the authority of Scripture confirmed by God with miracles: since we believe not what is above human reason save because God has revealed it. In support, however, of this kind of truth, certain probable arguments must be adduced for the practice and help of the faithful, but not for the conviction of our opponents,

20 because the very insufficiency of these arguments would rather confirm them in their error, if they thought that we assented to the truth of faith on account of such weak reasonings.

With the intention then of proceeding in the manner laid down, we shall first of all endeavour to declare that truth which is

25 the object of faith's confession and of reason's researches, by adducing arguments both demonstrative and probable, some of which we have gathered from the writings of the philosophers and of holy men, so as thereby to confirm the truth and convince our opponents. After this, so as to proceed from the more to the less

30 manifest, we shall with God's help proceed to declare that truth which surpasses reason, by refuting the arguments of our opponents, and by setting forth the truth of faith by means of probable arguments and authority.

Seeing then that we intend by the way of reason to pursue

35 those things about God which human reason is able to investigate, the first object that offers itself to our consideration consists in those things which pertain to God in Himself; the second will be the procession of creatures from Him; and the third the relation of creatures to Him as their end. Of those things which we need to

40 consider about God in Himself, we must give the first place (this being the necessary foundation of the whole of this work), to the

question of demonstrating that there is a God: for unless this be
established, all questions about divine things are out of court.

5

CHAPTER X

OF THE OPINION OF THOSE WHO AVER THAT IT CANNOT BE DEMONSTRATED THAT THERE IS A GOD, SINCE THIS IS SELF-EVIDENT

10

POSSIBLY it will seem to some that it is useless to endeavour
to show that there is a God: they say that it is self-evident that God
is, so that it is impossible to think the contrary, and thus it cannot
be demonstrated that there is a God. The reasons for this view are
15 as follow. Those things are said to be self-evident which are
known as soon as the terms are known: thus as soon as it is known
what is a whole, and what is a part, it is known that the whole is
greater than its part. Now such is the statement God is. For by this
word God we understand a thing a greater than which cannot be
20 thought of: this is what a man conceives in his mind when he hears
and understands this word God: so that God must already be at
least in his mind. Nor can He be in the mind alone, for that which
is both in the mind and in reality is greater than that which is in the
mind only. And the very signification of the word shows that
25 nothing is greater than God. Wherefore it follows that it is self-
evident that God is, since it is made clear from the very
signification of the word.

Again. It is possible to think that there is a thing which cannot
be thought not to exist: and such a thing is evidently greater than
30 that which can be thought not to exist. Therefore if God can be
thought not to exist, it follows that something can be thought
greater than God: and this is contrary to the signification of the
term. Therefore it remains that it is self-evident that God is.

Further. Those propositions are most evident in which the
35 selfsame thing is predicated of itself, for instance: Man is man; or
wherein the predicate is included in the definition of the subject,
for instance: Man is an animal. Now, as we shall show further on,
in God alone do we find that His being is His essence, as though
the same were the answer to the question, What is He? as to the
40 question, Is He? Accordingly when we say, God is, the predicate is
either identified with the subject, or at least is included in the

definition of the subject. And thus it will be self-evident that God is.

Moreover. Things that are known naturally are self-evident, for it is not by a process of research that they become evident.
5 Now it is naturally known that God is, since man's desire tends naturally to God as his last end, as we shall show further on. Therefore it is self-evident that God is.

Again. That whereby all things are known must needs be self-evident. Now such is God. For just as the light of the sun is the
10 principle of all visual perception, so the divine light is the principle of all intellectual knowledge, because it is therein that first and foremost intellectual light is to be found. Therefore it must needs be self-evident that God is.

On account of these and like arguments some are of opinion
15 that it is so self-evident that God is, that it is impossible for the mind to think the contrary.

CHAPTER XI

20

REFUTATION OF THE FOREGOING OPINION AND SOLUTION OF THE AFORESAID ARGUMENTS

THE foregoing opinion arose from their being accustomed from
25 the beginning to hear and call upon the name of God. Now custom, especially if it date from our childhood, acquires the force of nature, the result being that the mind holds those things with which it was imbued from childhood as firmly as though they were self-evident. It is also a result of failing to distinguish between
30 what is self-evident simply, and that which is self-evident to us. For it is simply self-evident that God is, because the selfsame thing which God is, is His existence. But since we are unable to conceive mentally the selfsame thing which is God, that thing remains unknown in regard to us. Thus it is self-evident simply
35 that every whole is greater than its part, but to one who fails to conceive mentally the meaning of a whole, it must needs be unknown. Hence it is that those things which are most evident of all are to the intellect what the sun is to the eye of an owl, as stated in *Metaph*. ii.
40 Nor does it follow, as the first argument alleged, that as soon as the meaning of the word God is understood, it is known that God is. First, because it is not known to all, even to those who

grant that there is a God, that God is that thing than which no greater can be thought of, since many of the ancients asserted that this world is God. Nor can any such conclusion be gathered from the significations which Damascene assigns to this word God.

5 Secondly because, granted that everyone understands this word God to signify something than which a greater cannot be thought of, it does not follow that something than which a greater cannot be thought of exists in reality. For we must needs allege a thing in the same way as we allege the signification of its name. Now from

10 the fact that we conceive mentally that which the word God is intended to convey, it does not follow that God is otherwise than in the mind. Wherefore neither will it follow that the thing than which a greater cannot be thought of is otherwise than in the mind. And thence it does not follow that there exists in reality

15 something than which a greater cannot be thought of. Hence this is no argument against those who assert that there is no God, since whatever be granted to exist, whether in reality or in the mind, there is nothing to prevent a person from thinking of something greater, unless he grants that there is in reality something than

20 which a greater cannot be thought of.

Again it does not follow, as the second argument pretended, that if it is possible to think that God is not, it is possible to think of something greater than God. For that it be possible to think that He is not, is not on account of the imperfection of His being or the

25 uncertainty thereof, since in itself His being is supremely manifest, but is the result of the weakness of our mind which is able to see Him, not in Himself but in His effects, so that it is led by reasoning to know that He is.

Wherefore the third argument also is solved. For just as it is

30 self-evident to us that a whole is greater than its part, so is it most evident to those who see the very essence of God that God exists, since His essence is His existence. But because we are unable to see His essence, we come to know His existence not in Himself but in His effects.

35 The solution to the fourth argument is also clear. For man knows God naturally in the same way as he desires Him naturally. Now man desires Him naturally in so far as he naturally desires happiness, which is a likeness of the divine goodness. Hence it does not follow that God considered in Himself is naturally known

40 to man, but that His likeness is. Wherefore man must needs come

by reasoning to know God in the likenesses to Him which he discovers in God's effects.

It is also easy to reply to the fifth argument. For God is that in which all things are known, not so that other things be unknown
5 except He be known, as happens in self-evident principles, but because all knowledge is caused in us by His outpouring.

CHAPTER XII

10

OF THE OPINION OF THOSE WHO SAY
THAT THE EXISTENCE OF GOD CANNOT BE PROVED,
AND THAT IT IS HELD BY FAITH ALONE

15 THE position that we have taken is also assailed by the opinion of certain others, whereby the efforts of those who endeavour to prove that there is a God would again be rendered futile. For they say that it is impossible by means of the reason to discover that God exists, and that this knowledge is acquired solely by means of
20 faith and revelation.

In making this assertion some were moved by the weakness of the arguments which certain people employed to prove the existence of God.

Possibly, however, this error might falsely seek support from
25 the statements of certain philosophers, who show that in God essence and existence are the same, namely that which answers to the question, What is He? and that which answers to the question, Is He? Now it is impossible by the process of reason to acquire the knowledge of what God is. Wherefore seemingly neither is it
30 possible to prove by reason whether God is.

Again. If, as required by the system of the Philosopher, in order to prove whether a thing is we must take as principle the signification of its name, and since according to the Philosopher (4 *Metaph.*) the signification of a name is its definition: there will
35 remain no means of proving the existence of God, seeing that we lack knowledge of the divine essence or quiddity.

Again. If the principles of demonstration become known to us originally through the senses, as is proved in the *Posterior Analytics*, those things which transcend all sense and sensible objects are
40 seemingly indemonstrable. Now such is the existence of God. Therefore it cannot be demonstrated.

The falseness of this opinion is shown to us first by the art of demonstration, which teaches us to conclude causes from effects. Secondly, by the order itself of sciences: for if no substance above sensible substance can be an object of science, there will be no
5   science above *Physics*, as stated in 4 *Metaph*. Thirdly, by the efforts of the philosophers who have endeavoured to prove the existence of God. Fourthly, by the apostolic truth which asserts (Rom. i. 20) that the invisible things of God are clearly seen, being understood by the things that are made.

10   Nor should we be moved by the consideration that in God essence and existence are the same, as the first argument contended. For this is to be understood of the existence by which God subsists in Himself, of which we are ignorant as to what kind of a thing it is, even as we are ignorant of His essence. But it is not
15   to be understood of that existence which is signified by the composition of the mind. For in this way it is possible to prove the existence of God, when our mind is led by demonstrative arguments to form a proposition stating that God is.

Moreover. In those arguments whereby we prove the
20   existence of God, it is not necessary that the divine essence or quiddity be employed as the middle term, as the second argument supposed: but instead of the quiddity we take His effects as middle term, as is the case in *a posteriori* reasoning: and from these effects we take the signification of this word God. For all the divine
25   names are taken either from the remoteness of God's effects from Himself, or from some relationship between God and His effects.

It is also evident from the fact that, although God transcends all sensibles and senses, His effects from which we take the proof that God exists, are sensible objects. Hence our knowledge, even
30   of things which transcend the senses, originates from the senses.

CHAPTER XIII

35   ARGUMENTS IN PROOF OF GOD'S EXISTENCE

HAVING shown then that it is not futile to endeavour to prove the existence of God, we may proceed to set forth the reasons whereby both philosophers and Catholic doctors have
40   proved that there is a God. In the first place we shall give the arguments by which Aristotle sets out to prove God's existence:

and he aims at proving this from the point of view of movement, in two ways.

   The first way is as follows. Whatever is in motion is moved by another: and it is clear to the sense that something, the sun for

5 instance, is in motion. Therefore it is set in motion by something else moving it. Now that which moves it is itself either moved or not. If it be not moved, then the point is proved that we must needs postulate an immovable mover: and this we call God. If, however, it be moved, it is moved by another mover. Either,

10 therefore, we must proceed to infinity, or we must come to an immovable mover. But it is not possible to proceed to infinity. Therefore it is necessary to postulate an immovable mover.

   This argument contains two propositions that need to be proved: namely that whatever is in motion is moved by another,

15 and that it is not possible to proceed to infinity in movers and things moved.

   The first of these is proved by the Philosopher in three ways. First, thus. If a thing moves itself, it must needs have the principle of its movement in itself, else it would clearly be moved by

20 another. Again it must be moved primarily, that is, it must be moved by reason of itself and not by reason of its part, as an animal is moved by the movement of its foot, for in the latter way not the whole but the part would be moved by itself, and one part by another. Again it must be divisible and have parts, since

25 whatever is moved is divisible, as is proved in 6 Phys.

   These things being supposed, he argues as follows. That which is stated to be moved by itself is moved primarily. Therefore if one of its parts is at rest, it follows that the whole is at rest. For if, while one part is at rest, another of its parts were in motion, the

30 whole itself would not be moved primarily, but its part which is in motion while another is at rest. Now nothing that is at rest while another is at rest, is moved by itself: for that which is at rest as a result of another thing being at rest must needs be in motion as a result of the other's motion, and hence it is not moved by itself.

35 Hence that which was stated to be moved by itself, is not moved by itself. Therefore whatever is in motion must needs be moved by another.

   Nor is this argument traversed by the statement that might be made, that supposing a thing moves itself, it is impossible for a

40 part thereof to be at rest, or again by the statement that to be at rest or in motion does not belong to a part except accidentally, as

Avicenna quibbles. Because the force of the argument lies in this, that if a thing moves itself primarily and of itself, not by reason of its parts, it follows that its being moved does not depend on some thing; whereas with a divisible thing, being moved, like being, depends on its parts, so that it cannot move itself primarily and of itself. Therefore the truth of the conclusion drawn does not require that we suppose as an absolute truth that a part of that which moves itself is at rest, but that this conditional statement be true that if a part were at rest, the whole would be at rest. Which statement can be true even if the antecedent be false, even as this conditional proposition is true: If a man is an ass he is irrational.

Secondly, he proves it by induction, thus. A thing is not moved by itself if it is moved accidentally, since its motion is occasioned by the motion of something else. Nor again if it is moved by force, as is manifest. Nor if it is moved by its nature like those things whose movement proceeds from themselves, such as animals, which clearly are moved by their souls. Nor if it is moved by nature, as heavy and light things are, since these are moved by their generating cause and by that which removes the obstacle to their movement. Now whatsoever things are in motion are moved either *per se* or accidentally; and if *per se*, either by force or by nature: and if the latter, either by something in them, as in the case of animals, or not by something in them, as in the case of heavy and light bodies. Therefore whatever is in motion is moved by another.

Thirdly, he proves his point thus. Nothing is at the same time in act and in potentiality in respect of the same thing. Now whatever is in motion, as such, is in potentiality, because motion is the act of that which is in potentiality, as such. Whereas whatever moves, as such, is in act, for nothing acts except in so far as it is in act. Therefore nothing is both mover and moved in respect of the same movement. Hence nothing moves itself.

We must observe, however, that Plato, who asserted that every mover is moved, employed the term movement in a more general sense than Aristotle. For Aristotle took movement in its strict sense, for the act of a thing that is in potentiality as such, in which sense it applies only to divisible things and bodies, as is proved in 6 *Phys.* Whereas according to Plato that which moves itself is not a body; for he took movement for any operation, so that to understand or to think is a kind of movement, to which manner of speaking Aristotle alludes in 3 *De Anima*. In this sense, then, he said that the first mover moves itself, in as much as it

understands, desires and loves itself. This, in a certain respect, is not in contradiction with the arguments of Aristotle; for it makes no difference whether with Plato we come to a first mover that moves itself, or with Aristotle to something first which is
5 altogether immovable.

He proves the other proposition, namely that it is impossible to proceed to infinity in movers and things moved, by three arguments.

The first of these is as follows. If one were to proceed to
10 infinity in movers and things moved, all this infinite number of things would necessarily be bodies, since whatever is moved is divisible and corporeal, as is proved in 6 *Phys.* Now every body that moves through being moved is moved at the same time as it moves. Therefore all this infinite number of things are moved at
15 the same time as one of them is moved. But one of them, since it is finite, is moved in a finite time. Therefore all this infinite number of things are moved in a finite time. But this is impossible. Therefore it is impossible to proceed to infinity in movers and things moved.
20 That it is impossible for the aforesaid infinite number of things to be moved in a finite time, he proves thus. Mover and moved must needs be simultaneous; and he proves this by induction from each species of movement. But bodies cannot be simultaneous except by continuity or contact. Wherefore since all the aforesaid
25 movers and things moved are bodies, as proved, they must needs be as one movable thing through their continuity or contact. And thus one infinite thing would be moved in a finite time, which is shown to be impossible in 6 *Phys.*

The second argument in proof of the same statement is as
30 follows. In an ordinate series of movers and things moved, where namely throughout the series one is moved by the other, we must needs find that if the first mover be taken away or cease to move, none of the others will move or be moved: because the first is the cause of movement in all the others. Now if an ordinate series of
35 movers and things moved proceed to infinity, there will be no first mover, but all will be intermediate movers as it were. Therefore it will be impossible for any of them to be moved: and thus nothing in the world will be moved.

The third argument amounts to the same, except that it
40 proceeds in the reverse order, namely by beginning from above: and it is as follows. That which moves instrumentally, cannot move unless there be something that moves principally. But if we

proceed to infinity in movers and things moved, they will all be like instrumental movers, because they will be alleged to be moved movers, and there will be nothing by way of principal mover. Therefore nothing will be moved.

5   We have thus clearly proved both statements which were supposed in the first process of demonstration whereby Aristotle proved the existence of a first immovable mover.

The second way is as follows. If every mover is moved, this statement is true either in itself or accidentally. If accidentally, it

10   follows that it is not necessary: for that which is accidentally true is not necessary. Therefore it is a contingent proposition that no mover is moved. But if a mover be not moved, it does not move, as the opponent asserts. Therefore it is contingent that nothing is moved, since, if nothing moves, nothing is moved. Now Aristotle

15   holds this to be impossible, namely, that at any time there be no movement. Therefore the first proposition was not contingent, because a false impossibility does not follow from a false contingency. And therefore this proposition, Every mover is moved by another, was not accidentally true.

20   Again, if any two things are found accidentally united in a certain subject, and one of them is to be found without the other, it is probable that the latter can be found without the former: thus if white and musical are found in Socrates, and musical without white is found in Plato, it is probable that it is possible to find

25   white without musical in some subject. Accordingly if mover and moved be united together in some subject accidentally, and it be found that a certain thing is moved without its being a mover, it is probable that a mover is to be found that is not moved. Nor can one urge against this the case of two things one of which depends

30   on the other; because those in question are united not *per se* but accidentally. If, however, the aforesaid proposition is true in itself, again there follows something impossible or unfitting. For the mover must needs be moved either by the same kind of movement or by another kind. If by the same kind, it follows that whatever

35   causes alteration must itself be altered, and furthermore that the healer must be healed, that the teacher must be taught, and in respect of the same science. But this is impossible: for the teacher must needs have science, while the learner must needs not have it, and thus the same will be both possessed and not possessed by the

40   same, which is impossible. And if it be moved by another kind of movement, so that, to wit, that which causes alteration be moved in respect of place, and that which moves in respect of place be

increased, and so on, it will follow that we cannot go on indefinitely, since the genera and species of movement are finite in number. And thus there will be some first mover that is not moved by another. Unless, perchance, someone say that a
5 recurrence takes place, in this way, that when all the genera and species of movement have been exhausted, a return must be made to the first; for instance, if that which moves in respect of place be altered, and that which causes alteration be increased, then again that which is increased be moved in respect of place. But the
10 consequence of this will be the same as before; namely, that which moves by one kind of movement is itself moved by the same kind, not immediately indeed but mediately. It remains therefore that we must needs postulate some first mover that is not moved by anything outside itself.

15   Since however, given that there is a first mover that is not moved by anything outside itself, it does not follow that it is absolutely immovable, Aristotle proceeds further, saying that this may happen in two ways. First, so that this first mover is absolutely immovable. And if this be granted, our point is
20 established, namely that there is a first immovable mover. Secondly, that this first mover is moved by itself. And this seems probable: because what is of itself is always prior to what is of another: wherefore also in things moved, it is logical that what is moved first is moved by itself and not by another.

25   But, if this be granted, the same consequence follows. For it cannot be said that the whole of that which moves itself is moved by its whole self, because then the absurd consequences mentioned above would follow, namely that a person might teach and be taught at the same time, and in like manner as to other
30 kinds of movement; and again that a thing would be at the same time in act and in potentiality, since a mover, as such, is in act, while that which is moved is in potentiality. It remains, therefore, that one part thereof is mover only, and the other part moved. And thus we have the same conclusion as before, namely that
35 there is something that moves and is itself immovable.

     And it cannot be said that both parts are moved, so that one is moved by the other; nor that one part moves both itself and the other; nor that the whole moves a part; nor that part moves the whole, since the above absurdities would follow, namely that
40 something would both move and be moved by the same kind of movement, and that it would be at the same time in potentiality and in act, and moreover that the whole would move itself not

primarily but by reason of its part. It remains, therefore, that in that which moves itself, one part must be immovable, and must move the other part.

Since, however, in those things among us which move themselves, namely animals, the part which moves, namely the soul, though immovable of itself, is nevertheless moved accidentally, he goes on to show that in the first mover, the part which moves is not moved neither of itself nor accidentally.

For in those things which among us move themselves, namely animals, since they are corruptible, the part which moves is moved accidentally. Now those corruptible things which move themselves must needs be reducible to some first self-mover that is everlasting. Therefore that which moves itself must have a mover, which is moved neither of itself nor accidentally.

It is clear that, in accordance with his hypothesis, some self-mover must be everlasting. For if, as he supposes, movement is everlasting, the production of these self-movers that are subject to generation and corruption must be everlasting. But no one of these self-movers, since it does not always exist, can be the cause of this everlastingness. Nor can all of them together, both because they would be infinite, and because they do not exist all together. It follows therefore that there must be an everlasting self-mover, that causes the everlastingness of generation in these lower self-movers. And thus its mover is not moved, neither of itself nor accidentally. Again, we observe that in self-movers some begin to be moved anew on account of some movement whereby the animal is not moved by itself, for instance by the digestion of food or a change in the atmosphere: by which movement the mover that moves itself is moved accidentally. Whence we may gather that no self-mover, whose mover is moved *per se* or accidentally, is always moved. But the first self-mover is always in motion, else movement could not be everlasting, since every other movement is caused by the movement of the first self-mover. It follows therefore that the first self-mover is moved by a mover who is not moved, neither *per se* nor accidentally.

Nor is this argument rebutted by the fact that the movers of the lower spheres cause an everlasting movement, and yet are said to be moved accidentally. For they are said to be moved accidentally not by reason of themselves, but by reason of the things subject to their motion, which follow the motion of the higher sphere.

Since, however, God is not part of a self-mover, Aristotle goes on in his Metaphysics to trace from this motor that is part of a self-mover, another mover altogether separate, which is God. For since every self-mover is moved through its appetite, it follows
5   that the motor that is part of a self-mover, moves on account of the appetite for some appetible object. And this object is above the motor in moving, because the appetent is a moved mover, whereas the appetible is a mover altogether unmoved. Therefore there must needs be a first mover separate and altogether
10 immovable, and this is God.

Now two things would seem to weaken the above arguments. The first of these is that they proceed from the supposition of the eternity of movement, and among Catholics this is supposed to be false. To this we reply that the most effective way to prove God's
15 existence is from the supposition of the eternity of the world, which being supposed, it seems less manifest that God exists. For if the world and movement had a beginning, it is clear that we must suppose some cause to have produced the world and movement, because whatever becomes anew must take its origin
20 from some cause of its becoming, since nothing evolves itself from potentiality to act, or from non-being to being.

The second is that the aforesaid arguments suppose that the first moved thing, namely the heavenly body, has its motive principle in itself, whence it follows that it is animated: and by
25 many this is not granted.

To this we reply that if the first mover is not supposed to have its motive principle in itself, it follows that it is immediately moved by something altogether immovable. Hence also Aristotle draws this conclusion with an alternative, namely that either we
30 must come at once to a first mover immovable and separate, or to a self-mover from which again we come to a first mover immovable and separate.

The Philosopher proceeds in a different way in 2 *Metaph.* to show that it is impossible to proceed to infinity in efficient causes,
35 and that we must come to one first cause, and this we call God. This is how he proceeds. In all efficient causes following in order, the first is the cause of the intermediate cause, and the intermediate is the cause of the ultimate, whether the intermediate be one or several. Now if the cause be removed, that
40 which it causes is removed. Therefore if we remove the first the intermediate cannot be a cause. But if we go on to infinity in efficient causes, no cause will be first. Therefore all the others

which are intermediate will be removed. Now this is clearly false. Therefore we must suppose the existence of a first efficient cause: and this is God.

Another reason can be drawn from the words of Aristotle. For in 2 *Metaph.* he shows that those things which excel as true excel as beings: and in 4 *Metaph.* he shows that there is something supremely true, from the fact that we see that of two false things one is falser than the other, wherefore it follows that one also is truer than the other. Now this is by reason of approximation to that which is simply and supremely true. Wherefore we may further conclude that there is something that is supremely being. And this we call God.

Another argument in support of this conclusion is adduced by Damascene from the government of things: and the same reasoning is indicated by the Commentator in 2 *Phys.* It runs as follows. It is impossible for contrary and discordant things to accord in one order always or frequently except by someone's governance, whereby each and all are made to tend to a definite end. Now we see that in the world things of different natures accord in one order, not seldom and fortuitously, but always or for the most part. Therefore it follows that there is someone by whose providence the world is governed. And this we God.

CHAPTER XIV

THAT IN ORDER TO ACQUIRE KNOWLEDGE OF GOD IT IS NECESSARY TO PROCEED BY THE WAY OF REMOTION

ACCORDINGLY having proved that there is a first being which we call God, it behoves us to inquire into His nature.

Now in treating of the divine essence the principal method to be followed is that of remotion. For the divine essence by its immensity surpasses every form to which our intellect reaches; and thus we cannot apprehend it by knowing what it is. But we have some knowledge thereof by knowing what it is not: and we shall approach all the nearer to the knowledge thereof according as we shall be enabled to remove by our intellect a greater number of things therefrom. For the more completely we see how a thing differs from others, the more perfectly we know it: since each thing has in itself its own being distinct from all other things. Wherefore when we know the definition of a thing, first we place it in a genus, whereby we know in general what it is, and afterwards we add differences, so as to mark its distinction from other things: and thus we arrive at the complete knowledge of a thing's essence.

5   Since, however, we are unable in treating of the divine essence to take what as a genus, nor can we express its distinction from other things by affirmative differences, we must needs express it by negative differences. Now just as in affirmative differences one restricts another, and brings us the nearer to a
10 complete description of the thing, according as it makes it to differ from more things, so one negative difference is restricted by another that marks a distinction from more things. Thus, if we say that God is not an accident, we thereby distinguish Him from all accidents; then if we add that He is not a body, we shall distinguish
15 Him also from certain substances, and thus in gradation He will be differentiated by suchlike negations from all beside Himself: and then when He is known as distinct from all things, we shall arrive at a proper consideration of Him. It will not, however, be perfect, because we shall not know what He is in Himself.

20   Wherefore in order to proceed about the knowledge of God by the way of remotion, let us take as principle that which is already made manifest by what we have said above, namely that God is altogether unchangeable. This is also confirmed by the authority of Holy Writ. For it is said (Malach. iii. 6): I am God
25 (Vulg., the Lord) and I change not; (James i. 17): With Whom there is no change; and (Num. xxiii. 19): God is not as a man . . . that He should be changed.

30   **CHAPTER XV**

THAT GOD IS ETERNAL

FROM the foregoing it is also clear that God is eternal.
35   For whatever begins or ceases to be, suffers this through movement or change. Now it has been shown that God is altogether unchangeable. Therefore He is eternal, having neither beginning nor end.

     Again. Only things which are moved are measured by time:
40 because time is the measure of movement, as stated in 4 Phys. Now God is absolutely without movement, as we have already proved. Therefore we cannot mark before and after in Him.

Therefore in Him there is not being after non-being, nor can He have non-being after being, nor is it possible to find any succession in His being, because these things cannot be understood apart from time. Therefore He is without beginning and end, and has all
5 His being simultaneously: and in this consists the notion of eternity.

Moreover. If anywhen He was not and afterwards was, He was brought by someone out of non-being into being. Not by Himself; because what is not cannot do anything. And if by
10 another, this other is prior to Him. Now it has been shown that God is the first cause. Therefore He did not begin to be. Therefore neither will He cease to be: because that which always was, has the power to be always. Therefore He is eternal.

Furthermore. We observe that in the world there are certain
15 things which can be and not be, namely those that are subject to generation and corruption. Now whatsoever is possible to be has a cause, because, as in itself it is equally related to two things, namely being and not being, it follows that if it acquires being this is the result of some cause. But, as proved above by Aristotle's
20 argument, we cannot go on to infinity in causes. Therefore we must suppose some thing, which it is necessary to be. Now every necessary thing either has a cause of its necessity from without, or has no such cause, but is necessary of itself. But we cannot go on to infinity in necessary things that have causes of their necessity
25 from without. Therefore we must suppose some first necessary thing which is necessary of itself: and this is God, since He is the first cause, as proved above. Therefore God is eternal, since whatever is necessary of itself is eternal.

Again. Aristotle proves the everlastingness of movement
30 from the everlastingness of time: and thence he goes on to prove the everlastingness of the substance that is the cause of movement. Now the first moving substance is God. Therefore He is everlasting. And supposing the everlastingness of time and movement to be denied, there still remains the argument in proof
35 of the everlastingness of substance. For if movement had a beginning, it must have had its beginning from some mover. And if this mover had a beginning, it had its beginning from some agent. And thus either we shall go on to infinity, or we shall come to something without a beginning.
40 Divine authority bears witness to this truth: wherefore the Psalm reads: But Thou, O Lord, endurest for ever, and again: But Thou art always the self-same, and Thy years shall not fail.

CHAPTER XVI

5   THAT IN GOD THERE IS NO PASSIVE POTENTIALITY

Now if God is eternal, it follows of necessity that He is not in potentiality.

For everything in whose substance there is an admixture of
10 potentiality, is possibly non-existent as regards whatever it has of potentiality, for that which may possibly be may possibly not be. Now God in Himself cannot not be, since He is eternal. Therefore in God there is no potentiality to be.

Again. Although that which is sometimes potential and
15 sometimes actual, is in point of time potential before being actual, nevertheless actuality is simply before potentiality: because potentiality does not bring itself into actuality, but needs to be brought into actuality by something actual. Therefore whatever is in any way potential has something previous to it. Now God is the
20 first being and the first cause, as stated above. Therefore in Him there is no admixture of potentiality.

Again. That which of itself must necessarily be, can nowise be possibly, since what of itself must be necessarily, has no cause, whereas whatever can be possibly, has a cause, as proved above.
25 Now God, in Himself, must necessarily be. Therefore nowise can He be possibly. Therefore no potentiality is to be found in His essence.

Again. Everything acts according as it is actual. Wherefore that which is not wholly actual acts, not by its whole self, but by
30 part of itself. Now that which does not act by its whole self is not the first agent, since it acts by participation of something and not by its essence. Therefore the first agent, which is God, has no admixture of potentiality, but is pure act.

Moreover. Just as it is natural that a thing should act in so far
35 as it is actual, so is it natural for it to be passive in so far as it is in potentiality, for movement is the act of that which is in potentiality. Now God is altogether impassible and immovable, as stated above. Therefore in Him there is no potentiality, namely that which is passive.

40   Further. We notice in the world something that passes from potentiality to actuality. Now it does not reduce itself from potentiality to actuality, because that which is potential is not yet,

wherefore neither can it act. Therefore it must be preceded by something else whereby it can be brought from potentiality to actuality. And if this again passes from potentiality to actuality, it must be preceded by something else, whereby it can be brought
5 from potentiality to actuality. But we cannot go on thus to infinity. Therefore we must come to something that is wholly actual and nowise potential. And this we call God.

10 ## CHAPTER XVII

THAT IN GOD THERE IS NO MATTER

FROM this it follows that God is not matter.
15 For matter, such as it is, is in potentiality.

Again. Matter is not a principle of activity: wherefore, as the Philosopher puts it, efficient and material causes do not coincide. Now, as stated above, it belongs to God to be the first efficient cause of things. Therefore He is not matter.
20 Moreover. For those who referred all things to matter as their first cause, it followed that natural things exist by chance: and against these it is argued in 2 *Phys*. Therefore if God, Who is the first cause, is the material cause of things, it follows that all things exist by chance.
25 Further. Matter does not become the cause of an actual thing, except by being altered and changed. Therefore if God is immovable, as proved above, He can nowise be a cause of things as their matter.

The Catholic faith professes this truth, asserting that God
30 created all things not out of His substance, but out of nothing.

The ravings of David of Dinant are hereby confounded, who dared to assert that God is the same as primary matter, because if they were not the same, they would needs differ by certain differences, and thus they would not be simple: since in that which
35 differs from another thing by a difference, the very difference argues composition. Now this proceeded from his ignorance of the distinction between difference and diversity. For as laid down in 10 *Metaph*. a thing is said to be different in relation to something, because whatever is different, differs by something, whereas
40 things are said to be diverse absolutely from the fact that they are not the same thing. Accordingly we must seek for a difference in things which have something in common, for we have to point to

something in them whereby they differ: thus two species have a common genus, wherefore they must needs be distinguished by differences. But in those things which have nothing in common, we have not to seek in what they differ, for they are diverse by
5   themselves. For thus are opposite differences distinguished from one another, because they do not participate in a genus as a part of their essence: and consequently we must not ask in what they differ, for they are diversified by their very selves. Thus too, God and primary matter are distinguished, since, the one being pure
10 act and the other pure potentiality, they have nothing in common.

CHAPTER XVIII

15   THAT IN GOD THERE IS NO COMPOSITION

FROM the foregoing we are able to conclude that there is no composition in God. For in every composite thing there must needs be act and potentiality: since several things cannot become
20 one simply, unless there be something actual there and something else potential. Because those things that are actually, are not united except as an assemblage or group, which are not one simply. In these moreover the very parts that are gathered together are as a potentiality in relation to the union: for they are
25 actually united after being potentially unitable. But in God there is no potentiality. Therefore in Him there is no composition.

Again. Every composite is subsequent to its components. Therefore the first being, namely God, has no component parts.

Further. Every composite is potentially dissoluble, so far as its
30 composite nature is concerned, although in some there is something else incompatible with dissolution. Now that which is dissoluble is in potentiality to not-being. But this cannot be said of God, since of His very essence He is necessarily. Therefore there is no composition in Him.

35   Moreover. Every composition requires a compounder: for if there be composition, it results from several things: and things that are several in themselves would not combine together unless they were united by a compounder. If then God were composite, He would have a compounder: for He could not compound
40 Himself, since no thing is its own cause, for it would precede itself, which is impossible. Now the compounder is the efficient cause of the composite. Therefore God would have an efficient

cause: and thus He would not be the first cause, which was proved above.

Again. In any genus the more simple a thing is the more excellent it is; such, in the genus hot, is fire which has no
5 admixture of cold. Therefore that which obtains the summit of nobility among beings, must be in the summit of simplicity. Now that which obtains the summit of nobility in things is what we call God, since He is the first cause, because the cause is more excellent than its effect. Therefore there can be no composition in
10 Him.

Moreover. In every composite thing the good does not belong to this or that part but to the whole, and I speak of good in reference to that goodness which is proper to, and is the perfection of, the whole: thus the parts are imperfect in relation to
15 the whole: thus the parts of a man are not a man, nor have the parts of the number six the perfection of six, nor do the parts of a line attain to the perfection of the measure found in the whole line. Therefore if God is composite, His proper perfection and goodness are found in the whole of God but not in any of His
20 parts. And thus the good that is proper to Him will not be purely in Him; and consequently He will not be the first and supreme good.

Further. Before every multitude it is necessary to find unity. Now in every composite there is multitude. Therefore that which
25 is before all things, namely God, must needs be devoid of all composition.

THIRD BOOK
[On Providence]

CHAPTER I

FOREWORD

The Lord is a great God and a great King above all gods. For the Lord
will not reject His people. For in His hands are all the ends of the earth
and the heights of the mountains are His. For the sea is His and He made
5 *it, and His hands formed the dry land* (Ps. xciv. 3 seqq.)

WE have shown in the preceding books that there is one First
Being, possessing the full perfection of all being, whom we call
God, and who of the abundance of His perfection, bestows being
10 on all that exists, so that He is proved to be not only the first of
beings, but also the beginning of all. Moreover He bestows being
on others, not through natural necessity, but according to the
decree of His will, as we have shown above. Hence it follows that
He is the Lord of the things made by Him: since we dominate over
15 those things that are subject to our will. And this is a perfect
dominion that He exercises over things made by Him, forasmuch
as in their making He needs neither the help of an extrinsic agent,
nor matter as the foundation of His work: since He is the universal
efficient cause of all being.

20   Now everything that is produced through the will of an agent
is directed to an end by that agent: because the good and the end
are the proper object of the will, wherefore whatever proceeds
from a will must needs be directed to an end. And each thing
attains its end by its own action, which action needs to be directed
25 by him who endowed things with the principles whereby they act.

Consequently God, who in Himself is perfect in every way,
and by His power endows all things with being, must needs be the
Ruler of all, Himself ruled by none: nor is any thing to be
excepted from His ruling, as neither is there any thing that does
30 not owe its being to Him. Therefore as He is perfect in being and
causing, so is He perfect in ruling.

The effect of this ruling is seen to differ in different things,
according to the difference of natures. For some things are so
produced by God that, being intelligent, they bear a resemblance

to Him and reflect His image: wherefore not only are they directed, but they direct themselves to their appointed end by their own actions. And if in thus directing themselves they be subject to the divine ruling, they are admitted by that divine ruling
5 to the attainment of their last end; but are excluded therefrom if they direct themselves otherwise.

Others there are, bereft of intelligence, which do not direct themselves to their end, but are directed by another. Of these some being incorruptible, even as they are not patient of defect in
10 their natural being, so neither do they wander, in their own action, from the direction to their appointed end, but are subject, without fail, to the ruling of the supreme ruler; such are the heavenly bodies, whose movements are invariable. Others, however, being corruptible, are patient of defects in their natural
15 being; yet this defect is supplied to the advantage of another: since when one thing is corrupted, another is generated. Likewise, they fail from their natural direction in their own actions, yet this failing is compensated by some resultant good. Whence it is clear that not even those things which are seen to wander from the
20 direction of the supreme ruling, escape from the power of the supreme ruler: because also these corruptible bodies, even as they are created by God, so too are they perfectly subject to Him. Wherefore, considering this, the Psalmist, filled with the divine spirit, in order to give us an illustration of the divine government,
25 first describes to us the perfection of the supreme governor,—as to His nature when he says, God: as to His power, when he says, a great Lord, implying that He needs no one for His power to produce its effect: as to His authority, when he says, A great king above all gods, since, although there be many rulers, yet are all
30 subject to His rule. Secondly, he describes to us the manner of this government. As regards intellectual beings, which, if they submit to His rule, receive from Him their last end which is Himself; wherefore he says, For the Lord will not reject His people. As regards things corruptible which, albeit at times they wander from
35 their proper mode of action, never escape the power of the supreme ruler, he says, Because in His hands are all the ends of the earth. And as regards the heavenly bodies, which transcend the highest summits of the earth, that is of corruptible bodies, and always maintain the order of the divine government, he says, And
40 the mountain heights are His. Thirdly, he assigns the reason of this universal government, for the things that God made must needs be

governed by Him. To this he refers when he says, For the sea is
His, etc.

Since then in the First Book we have treated of the perfection
of the divine nature, and, in the Second, of the perfection of the
5 divine power, inasmuch as He is the creator and lord of all: it
remains for us in this Third Book to treat of His perfect authority
or dignity, inasmuch as He is the end and governor of all. We
must therefore proceed in this wise, so as first to treat of Him as
the end of all things; secondly of His universal government,
10 inasmuch as He governs every creature: thirdly, of that special
government, whereby He governs creatures endowed with
intelligence.

15 **CHAPTER II**

THAT EVERY AGENT ACTS FOR AN END

ACCORDINGLY we must first show that every agent, by its
20 action, intends an end.

For in those things which clearly act for an end, we declare
the end to be that towards which the movement of the agent
tends: for when this is reached, the end is said to be reached, and
to fail in this is to fail in the end intended; as may be seen in the
25 physician who aims at health, and in a man who runs towards an
appointed goal. Nor does it matter, as to this, whether that which
tends to an end be cognitive or not: for just as the target is the end
of the archer, so is it the end of the arrow's flight. Now the
movement of every agent tends to something determinate: since it
30 is not from any force that any action proceeds, but heating
proceeds from heat, and cooling from cold; wherefore actions are
differentiated by their active principles. Action sometimes
terminates in something made, for instance building terminates in
a house, healing ends in health: while sometimes it does not so
35 terminate, for instance, understanding and sensation. And if action
terminate in something made, the movement of the agent tends by
that action towards that thing made: while if it does not terminate
in something made, the movement of the agent tends to the action
itself. It follows therefore that every agent intends an end while
40 acting, which end is sometimes the action itself, sometimes a thing
made by the action.

Again. In all things that act for an end, that is said to be the last end, beyond which the agent seeks nothing further: thus the physician's action goes as far as health, and this being attained, his efforts cease. But in the action of every agent, a point can be
5   reached beyond which the agent does not desire to go; else actions would tend to infinity, which is impossible; for since it is not possible to pass through an infinite medium, the agent would never begin to act, because nothing moves towards what it cannot reach. Therefore every agent acts for an end.

10   Moreover. If the actions of an agent proceed to infinity, these actions must needs result either in something made, or not. If the result is something made, the being of that thing made will follow after an infinity of actions. But that which presupposes an infinity of things, cannot possibly be, since an infinite medium cannot be
15   passed through. Now impossibility of being argues impossibility of becoming: and that which cannot become, it is impossible to make. Therefore it is impossible for an agent to begin to make a thing for the making of which an infinity of actions are presupposed.—If, however, the result of such actions be not
20   something made, the order of these actions must be either according to the order of active forces, (for instance if a man feel that he may imagine, and imagine that he may understand, and understand that he may will): or according to the order of objects, (for instance I consider the body that I may consider the soul,
25   which I consider in order to consider a separate substance, which again I consider so that I may consider God). Now it is not possible to proceed to infinity, either in active forces, as neither is this possible in the forms of things, as proved in 2 *Metaph.*, since the form is the principle of activity: or in objects, as neither is this
30   possible in beings, since there is one first being, as we have proved above. Therefore it is not possible for agents to proceed to infinity: and consequently there must be something, which being attained, the efforts of the agent cease. Therefore every agent acts for an end.

35   Further. In things that act for an end, whatsoever comes between the first agent and the last end, is an end in respect to what precedes, and an active principle in respect of what follows. Hence if the effort of the agent does not tend to something determinate, and if its action, as stated, proceeds to infinity, the
40   active principles must needs proceed to infinity: which is impossible, as we have shown above. Therefore the effort of the agent must of necessity tend to something determinate.

Again. Every agent acts either by nature or by intelligence. Now there can be no doubt that those which act by intelligence act for an end; since they act with an intellectual preconception of what they attain by their action, and act through such
5 preconception, for this is to act by intelligence. Now just as in the preconceiving intellect there exists the entire likeness of the effect that is attained by the action of the intellectual being, so in the natural agent there pre-exists the similitude of the natural effect, by virtue of which similitude its action is determined to the
10 appointed effect: for fire begets fire, and an olive produces an olive. Wherefore even as that which acts by intelligence tends by its action to a definite end, so also does that which acts by nature. Therefore every agent acts for an end.

Moreover. Fault is not found save in those things which are
15 for an end: for we do not find fault with one who fails in that to which he is not appointed; thus we find fault with a physician if he fail to heal, but not with a builder or a grammarian. But we find fault in things done according to art, as when a grammarian fails to speak correctly; and in things that are ruled by nature, as in the
20 case of monstrosities. Therefore every agent, whether according to nature, or according to art, or acting of set purpose, acts for an end.

Again. Were an agent not to act for a definite effect, all effects would be indifferent to it. Now that which is indifferent to many
25 effects does not produce one rather than another: wherefore from that which is indifferent to either of two effects, no effect results, unless it be determined by something to one of them. Hence it would be impossible for it to act. Therefore every agent tends to some definite effect, which is called its end.

30 There are, however, certain actions which would seem not to be for an end, such as playful and contemplative actions, and those which are done without attention, such as scratching one's beard, and the like: whence some might be led to think that there is an agent that acts not for an end. But we must observe that
35 contemplative actions are not for another end, but are themselves an end. Playful actions are sometimes an end, when one plays for the mere pleasure of play; and sometimes they are for an end, as when we play that afterwards we may study better. Actions done without attention do not proceed from the intellect, but from
40 some sudden act of the imagination, or some natural principle: thus a disordered humour produces an itching sensation and is the cause of a man scratching his beard, which he does without his

mind attending to it. Such actions do tend to an end, although outside the order of the intellect. Hereby is excluded the error of certain natural philosophers of old, who maintained that all things happen by natural necessity, thus utterly banishing the final cause
5 from things.

CHAPTER III

10   THAT EVERY AGENT ACTS FOR A GOOD

HENCE we must go on to prove that every agent acts for a good.

For that every agent acts for an end clearly follows from the
15 fact that every agent tends to something definite. Now that to which an agent tends definitely must needs be befitting to that agent: since the latter would not tend to it save on account of some fittingness thereto. But that which is befitting to a thing is good for it. Therefore every agent acts for a good.

20   Further. The end is that wherein the appetite of the agent or mover is at rest, as also the appetite of that which is moved. Now it is the very notion of good to be the term of appetite, since good is the object of every appetite. Therefore all action and movement is for a good.

25   Again. All action and movement would seem to be directed in some way to being: either for the preservation of being in the species or in the individual; or for the acquisition of being. Now this itself, being to wit, is a good: and for this reason all things desire being. Therefore all action and movement is for a good.

30   Furthermore. All action and movement is for some perfection. For if the action itself be the end, it is clearly a second perfection of the agent. And if the action consist in the transformation of external matter, clearly the mover intends to induce some perfection into the thing moved: towards which
35 perfection the movable tends, if the movement be natural. Now when we say a thing is perfect, we mean that it is good. Therefore every action and movement is for a good.

Also. Every agent acts according as it is actual. Now by acting it tends to something similar to itself. Therefore it tends to an act.
40 But an act has the ratio of good: since evil is not found save in a potentiality lacking act. Therefore every action is for a good.

Moreover. The intellectual agent acts for an end, as determining on its end: whereas the natural agent, though it acts for an end, as proved above, does not determine on its end, since it knows not the ratio of end, but is moved to the end determined
5 for it by another. Now an intellectual agent does not determine the end for itself except under the aspect of good; for the intelligible object does not move except it be considered as a good, which is the object of the will. Therefore also the natural agent is not moved, nor does it act for an end, except in so far as
10 this end is a good, since the end is determined for the natural agent by an appetite. Therefore every agent acts for a good.

Again. To shun evil and to seek good are in the same ratio: even as movement from below and upward movement are in the same ratio. Now we observe that all things shun evil: for
15 intellectual agents shun a thing for the reason that they apprehend it as an evil: and all natural agents, in proportion to their strength, resist corruption which is the evil of everything. Therefore all things act for a good.

Again. That which results from the agent's action beside his
20 intention, is said to happen by chance or luck. Now we observe in the works of nature that either always or more often that happens which is best: thus in plants the leaves are so placed as to protect the fruit; and the parts of an animal are so disposed as to conduce to the animal's safety. Wherefore, if this happens beside the
25 intention of the natural agent, it will be the result of chance or luck. But that is impossible: because things that happen always or frequently, are not casual or fortuitous, but those which occur seldom. Therefore the natural agent tends to that which is best: and much more evidently is this so with the intellectual agent.
30 Therefore every agent intends a good in acting.

Moreover. Whatever is moved is brought to the term of movement by the mover and agent. Therefore mover and moved tend to the same term. Now that which is moved, since it is in potentiality, tends to an act, and consequently to perfection and
35 goodness: for by its movement it passes from potentiality to act. Therefore mover and agent by moving and acting always intend a good.

Hence the philosophers in defining the good said: The good is the object of every appetite; and Dionysius (*De Div. Nom.* iv.) says
40 that all things desire the good and the best.

*   *   *

CHAPTER XVI

THAT THE END OF EVERYTHING IS A GOOD

5

ACCORDINGLY if every agent acts for some good, as we have shown above, it follows that good is the end of each thing. For everything is directed by its action to some end; since either the action itself is an end; or the end of the action is also the end of
10 the agent: and this is its good.

Again. The end of a thing is the term of its appetite. Now the appetite of a thing terminates in a good: for the Philosopher defines good as the object of all appetite. Therefore the end of everything is a good.

15 Moreover. That toward which a thing tends while it is without it, and wherein it rests when it has it, is its end. Now anything that is without its proper perfection, is moved towards it, as far as in it lies: and if it have that perfection, it rests therein. Therefore the end of a thing is its perfection. But the perfection of
20 a thing is its good. Therefore every thing is directed to good as its end.

Further. Things that know the end, and things that do not know the end, are equally directed to the end: although those which know the end are moved thereto *per se*; whereas those
25 which do not know it, tend thereto as directed by another, as may be seen in the archer and the arrow. Now those that know the end, are always directed to a good as their end; because the will which is the appetite of a previously known end, does not tend towards a thing except under the aspect of good, which is its
30 object. Therefore also those things that do not know the end, are directed to a good as their end. Therefore the end of all is a good.

CHAPTER XVII

35

THAT ALL THINGS ARE DIRECTED TO ONE END, WHICH IS GOD

FROM the foregoing it is clear that all things are directed to
40 one good as their last end.

For if nothing tends to something as its end, except in so far as this is good, it follows that good, as such, is an end. Consequently that which is the supreme good is supremely the end of all. Now there is but one Supreme good, namely God, as we have shown in the First Book. Therefore all things are directed to the Supreme good, namely God, as their end.

5 Again. That which is supreme in any genus, is the cause of everything in that genus: thus fire which is supremely hot is the cause of heat in other bodies. Therefore the supreme good, namely God, is the cause of goodness in all things good. Therefore He is the cause of every end being an end: since whatever is an

10 end, is such, in so far as it is good. Now the cause of a thing being such, is yet more so. Therefore God is supremely the end of all things.

Further. In every series of causes, the first cause is more a cause than the second causes: since the second cause is not a cause

15 save through the first. Therefore that which is the first cause in the series of final causes, must needs be more the final cause of each thing, than the proximate final cause. Now God is the first cause in the series of final causes: for He is supreme in the order of good things. Therefore He is the end of each thing more even than any

20 proximate end.

Moreover. In all mutually subordinate ends the last must needs be the end of each preceding end: thus if a potion be mixed to be given to a sick man; and is given to him that he may be purged; and he be purged that he may be lowered, and lowered

25 that he may be healed, it follows that health is the end of the lowering, and of the purging, and of those that precede. Now all things are subordinate in various degrees of goodness to the one supreme good, that is the cause of all goodness: and so, since good has the aspect of an end, all things are subordinate to God as

30 preceding ends under the last end. Therefore God must be the end of all.

Furthermore. The particular good is directed to the common good as its end: for the being of the part is on account of the whole: wherefore the good of the nation is more godlike than the

35 good of one man. Now the supreme good, namely God, is the common good, since the good of all things depends on him: and the good whereby each thing is good, is the particular good of that thing, and of those that depend thereon. Therefore all things are directed to one good, God to wit, as their end.

40 Again. Order among ends is consequent to the order among agents: for just as the supreme agent moves all second agents, so must all the ends of second agents be directed to the end of the

supreme agent: since whatever the supreme agent does, it does for its own end. Now the supreme agent is the active principle of the actions of all inferior agents, by moving all to their actions, and consequently to their ends. Hence it follows that all the ends of
5 second agents are directed by the first agent to its proper end. Now the first agent in all things is God, as we proved in the Second Book. And His will has no other end but His own goodness, which is Himself, as we showed in the First Book. Therefore all things whether they were made by Him
10 immediately, or by means of secondary causes, are directed to God as their end. But this applies to all things: for as we proved in the Second Book, there can be nothing that has not its being from Him. Therefore all things are directed to God as their end.

Moreover. The last end of every maker, as such, is himself:
15 for what we make we use for our own sake: and if at any time a man make a thing for the sake of something else, it is referred to his own good, whether his use, his pleasure, or his virtue. Now God is the cause of all things being made; of some immediately, of others by means of other causes, as we have explained above.
20 Therefore He is the end of all things.

And again. The end holds the highest place among causes, and it is from it that all other causes derive their actual causality: since the agent acts not except for the end, as was proved. And it is due to the agent that the matter is brought to the actuality of the form:
25 wherefore the matter is made actually the matter, and the form is made the form, of this particular thing, through the agent's action, and consequently through the end. The later end also, is the cause of the preceding end being intended as an end: for a thing is not moved towards a proximate end, except for the sake of the last
30 end. Therefore the last end is the first cause of all. Now it must needs befit the First Being, namely God, to be the first cause of all, as we proved above. Therefore God is the last end of all.

Hence it is written (Prov. xvi. 13): The Lord hath made all things for himself: and (Apoc. xxii. 13), I am Alpha and Omega,
35 the first and the last.

CHAPTER XVIII

HOW GOD IS THE END OF THINGS

5   IT remains to ask how God is the end of all things: and this
shall be made clear from what has been said.

For He is the end of all things, yet so as to precede all in
being. Now there is an end which, though it holds the first place in
causing forasmuch as it is in the intention, is nevertheless last in
10   execution. This applies to any end which the agent sets up by his
action: thus the physician by his action sets up health in the sick
man, which is nevertheless his end. There is also an end which,
just as it precedes in causing, so also does it precede in being: even
so that which one intends to acquire by one's motion or action, is
15   said to be one's end, for instance fire seeks to reach a higher place
by its movement, and the king seeks to take a city by fighting.
Accordingly God is the end of things as something to be obtained
by each thing in its own way.

Again. God is at once the last end of things, and the first
20   agent, as we have shown. Now the end effected by the agent's
action, cannot be the first agent, but rather is it the agent's effect.
God, therefore, cannot be the end of things, as though He were
something effected, but only as something already existing and to
be acquired.

25   Further. If a thing act for the sake of something already in
existence, and if by its action some result ensue; something
through the agent's action must accrue to the thing for the sake of
which it acts: thus soldiers fight for the cause of their captain, to
whom victory accrues, which the soldiers bring about by their
30   actions. Now nothing can accrue to God from the action of
anything whatever: since His goodness is perfect in every way, as
we proved in the First Book. It follows, then, that God is the end
of things, not as something made or effected by them, nor as
though He obtained something from things, but in this way alone,
35   that things obtain Him.

Moreover, The effect must tend to the end, in the same way
as the agent acts for the end. Now God, who is the first agent of
all things, does not act as though He gained something by His
action, but as bestowing something thereby: since He is not in
40   potentiality so that He can acquire something, but solely in perfect
actuality, whereby He is able to bestow. Things therefore are not
directed to God, as to an end that can gain something, but that

they may obtain Himself from Him according to their measure, since He is their end.

CHAPTER XIX

THAT ALL THINGS TEND TO BE LIKE UNTO GOD

FROM the fact that they acquire the divine goodness,
10 creatures are made like unto God. Wherefore if all things tend to God as their last end, so as to acquire His goodness, it follows that the last end of things is to become like unto God.

Moreover. The agent is said to be the end of the effect forasmuch as the effect tends to be like the agent: wherefore the
15 form of the generator is the end of the act of generation. Now God is the end of things in such wise as to be also their first active cause. Therefore all things tend to a likeness to God, as their last end.

Again. Things give evidence that they naturally desire to be:
20 so that if any are corruptible, they naturally resist corruptives, and tend to where they can be safeguarded, as the fire tends upwards and earth downwards. Now all things have being in so far as they are like God, who is self-subsistent being: for they are beings only by participation. Therefore all things desire as their last end to be
25 like God.

Further. All creatures are images of the first agent, namely God: since the agent produces its like. Now the perfection of an image consists in representing the original by its likeness thereto: for this is why an image is made. Therefore all things are for the
30 purpose of acquiring a divine similitude, as their last end.

Again. Each thing by its movement or action tends to some good as its end, as proved above. Now a thing partakes of the good, in so far as it is like to the sovereign goodness, which is God. Therefore all things, by their movements and actions, tend
35 to a divine likeness as their last end.

*   *   *

CHAPTER XXV

THAT TO KNOW GOD IS THE END OF
EVERY INTELLIGENT SUBSTANCE

5

Now, seeing that all creatures, even those that are devoid of reason, are directed to God as their last end: and that all reach this end in so far as they have some share of a likeness to him: the intellectual creature attains to him in a special way, namely through its proper operation, by understanding him. Consequently this must be the end of the intelligent creature, namely to understand God.

For, as we have shown above, God is the end of each thing: wherefore as far as it is possible to it each thing intends to be united to God as its last end. Now a thing is more closely united to God by reaching in a way to the very substance of God; which happens when it knows something of the divine substance,—than when it reaches to a divine likeness. Therefore the intellectual substance tends to the knowledge of God as its last end.

Again. The operation proper to a thing is the end thereof: for it is its second perfection; so that when a thing is well conditioned for its proper operation it is said to be efficient and good. Now understanding is the proper operation of the intellectual substance: and consequently it is its end. Therefore whatever is most perfect in this operation, is its last end; especially in those operations which are not directed to some product, such as understanding and sensation. And since operations of this kind take their species from their objects, by which also they are known, it follows that the more perfect the object of any such operation, the more perfect is the operation. Consequently to understand the most perfect intelligible, namely God, is the most perfect in the genus of this operation which is to understand. Therefore to know God by an act of intelligence is the last end of every intellectual substance.

Someone, however, might say that the last end of an intellectual substance consists indeed in understanding the best intelligible: but that what is the best intelligible for this or that intellectual substance, is not simply the best intelligible; and that the higher the intellectual substance, the higher is its best intelligible. So that possibly the supreme intellectual substance has for its best intelligible that which is best simply, and its happiness will consist in understanding God: whereas the happiness of any

lower intellectual substance will consist in understanding some lower intelligible, which however will be the highest thing understood by that substance. Especially would it seem not to be in the power of the human intellect to understand that which is
5 simply the best intelligible, on account of its weakness: for it is as much adapted for knowing the supreme intelligible, as the owl's eye for seeing the sun.

Nevertheless it is evident that the end of any intellectual substance, even the lowest, is to understand God. For it has been
10 shown above that God is the last end towards which all things tend. And the human intellect, although the lowest in the order of intelligent substances, is superior to all that are devoid of understanding. Since then a more exalted substance has not a less exalted end, God will be the end also of the human intelligence.
15 Now every intelligent being attains to its last end by understanding it, as we have proved. Therefore the human intellect attains to God as its end, by understanding Him.

Again. Just as things devoid of intelligence tend to God as their end, by way of assimilation, so do intelligent substances by
20 way of knowledge, as clearly appears from what has been said. Now although things devoid of reason tend towards a likeness to their proximate causes, the intention of nature does not rest there, but has for its end a likeness to the sovereign good, as we have proved, although they are able to attain to this likeness in a most
25 imperfect manner. Therefore however little be the knowledge of God to which the intellect is able to attain, this will be the intellect's last end, rather than the perfect knowledge of lower intelligibles.

Moreover. Everything desires its last end most of all. Now the
30 human intellect desires, loves and enjoys the knowledge of divine things, although it can grasp but little about them, more than the perfect knowledge which it has of the lower world. Therefore man's last end is to understand God in some way or other.

Further. Everything tends to a divine likeness as its own end.
35 Therefore a thing's last end is that whereby it is most of all like unto God. Now the intellectual creature is especially likened to God in that it is intellectual: since this likeness belongs to it above other creatures, and includes all other likenesses. And in this particular kind of likeness it is more like God in understanding
40 actually than in understanding habitually or potentially: because God is always actually understanding, as we proved in the First Book. And in understanding actually he is especially like God, in

understanding God: because by understanding Himself God
understands all other things, as we proved in the First Book.
Therefore the last end of every intelligent substance is to
understand God.

5   Again. That which is lovable only on account of another, is for
the sake of that which is lovable for its own sake alone: because we
cannot go on indefinitely in the appetite of nature, since then
nature's desire would be in vain, for it is impossible to pass
through an infinite number of things. Now all practical sciences,
10   arts and powers are lovable only for the sake of something else,
since their end is not knowledge, but work. But speculative
sciences are lovable for their own sake, for their end is knowledge
itself. Nor can we find any action in connexion with man, that is
not directed to some other end, with the exception of speculative
15   consideration. For even playful actions, which would seem to be
done without any purpose, have some end due to them, namely
that the mind may be relaxed, and that thereby we may afterwards
become more fit for studious occupations: else we should always
have to be playing, if play were desirable for its own sake, and this
20   is unreasonable. Accordingly practical art is directed to speculative
art, and again every human operation, to intellectual speculation,
as its end. Now, in all sciences and arts that are mutually
subordinate, the last end apparently belongs to the one from
which others take their rules and principles: thus the art of sailing,
25   to which belongs the ship's end, namely its use, provides rules and
principles to the art of ship-building. And such is the relation of
metaphysics to other speculative sciences, for all others depend
thereon, since they derive their principles from it, and are
directed by it in defending those principles; moreover metaphysics
30   is wholly directed to God as its last end, wherefore it is called the
divine science. Therefore the knowledge of God is the last end of
all human knowledge and actions.

Furthermore. In all mutually subordinate agents and movers,
the end of the first agent must be the end of all: even as the end of
35   the commander in chief is the end of all who are soldiering under
him. Now of all the parts of man, the intellect is the highest
mover: for it moves the appetite, by proposing its object to it; and
the intellective appetite or will, moves the sensitive appetites,
namely the irascible and concupiscible, so that we do not obey the
40   concupiscence, unless the will command; and the sensitive
appetite, the will consenting, moves the body. Therefore the end
of the intellect is the end of all human actions. Now the intellect's

end and good are the true, and its last end is the first truth. Therefore the last end of all man and of all his deeds and desires, is to know the first truth, namely God.

Moreover. Man has a natural desire to know the causes of whatever he sees: wherefore through wondering at what they saw, and ignoring its cause, men first began to philosophize, and when they had discovered the cause they were at rest. Nor do they cease inquiring until they come to the first cause; and then do we deem ourselves to know perfectly when we know the first cause. Therefore man naturally desires, as his last end, to know the first cause. But God is the first cause of all. Therefore man's last end is to know God.

Besides. Man naturally desires to know the cause of any known effect. Now the human intellect knows universal being. Therefore it naturally desires to know its cause, which is God alone, as we proved in the Second Book. Now one has not attained to one's last end until the natural desire is at rest. Therefore the knowledge of any intelligible object is not enough for man's happiness, which is his last end, unless he know God also, which knowledge terminates his natural desire, as his last end. Therefore this very knowledge of God is man's last end.

Further. A body that tends by its natural appetite to its place, is moved all the more vehemently and rapidly, the nearer it approaches its end: wherefore Aristotle proves (I. *De Coel.* viii.) that a natural straight movement cannot be towards an indefinite point, because it would not be more moved afterwards than before. Hence that which tends more vehemently to a thing afterwards than before, is not moved towards an indefinite point but towards something fixed. Now this we find in the desire of knowledge: for the more one knows, the greater one's desire to know. Consequently man's natural desire in knowledge tends to a definite end. This can be no other but the highest thing knowable, which is God. Therefore the knowledge of God is man's last end.

Now the last end of man and of any intelligent substance is called happiness or beatitude: for it is this that every intelligent substance desires as its last end, and for its own sake alone. Therefore the last beatitude or happiness of any intelligent substance is to know God.

Hence it is said (Matth. v. 8): Blessed are the clean of heart, for they shall see God: and (Jo. xvii. 3): This is eternal life: that they may know thee, the only true God. Aristotle agrees with this statement (10 *Ethic.* vii.) when he says that man's ultimate happiness is contemplative, in regard to his contemplating the highest object of contemplation.

CHAPTER XXVI

DOES HAPPINESS CONSIST IN AN ACT OF THE WILL?

SINCE the intellectual substance attains to God by its operation, not only by an act of understanding but also by an act of the will, through desiring and loving Him, and through delighting in Him, someone might think that man's last end and ultimate happiness consists, not in knowing but in loving God or in some other act of the will towards Him: especially seeing that the object of the will is the good, which has the aspect of an end, whereas the true, which is the object of the intellect, has not the aspect of an end except forasmuch as it also is a good. Wherefore seemingly man does not attain to his last end by an act of his intellect, but rather by an act of his will.

Further. The ultimate perfection of operation is delight, which perfects operation as beauty perfects youth, as the Philosopher says (10 *Ethic.* iv.). Hence if the last end be a perfect operation, it would seem that it must consist in an act of the will rather than of the intellect.

Again. Delight apparently is desired for its own sake so that it is never desired for the sake of something else: for it is silly to ask of anyone why he seeks to be delighted. Now this is a condition of the ultimate end, namely that it be sought for its own sake. Therefore seemingly the last end consists in an act of the will rather than of the intellect.

Moreover. All agree in their desire for the last end, for it is a natural desire. Now more people seek delight than knowledge. Therefore delight would seem to be the last end rather than knowledge.

Furthermore. The will is seemingly a higher power than the intellect: for the will moves the intellect to its act; since when a person wills, his intellect considers by an act what he holds by a habit. Wherefore seemingly the act of the will is higher than the act of the intellect. Therefore it would seem that the last end, which is beatitude, consists in an act of the will rather than of the intellect.

But this can be clearly shown to be impossible. For since happiness is the proper good of the intellectual nature, it must needs become the intellectual nature according to that which is proper thereto. Now appetite is not proper to the intellectual
5 nature, but is in all things, although it is different in different things. This difference, however, arises from things having a different relation to knowledge. For things wholly devoid of knowledge have only a natural appetite: those that have a sensitive knowledge, have also a sensitive appetite, under which the
10 irascible and concupiscible appetites are comprised. And those which have intellective knowledge, have also an appetite proportionate to that knowledge, namely the will. The will therefore, forasmuch as it is an appetite, is not proper to the intellectual nature, but only in so far as it is dependent on the
15 intellect. On the other hand the intellect is in itself proper to the intellectual nature. Therefore beatitude or happiness consists principally and essentially in an act of the intellect, rather than in an act of the will.

Again. In all powers that are moved by their objects, the
20 object is naturally prior to the acts of those powers: even as the mover is naturally prior to the movable being moved. Now such a power is the will: for the appetible object moves the appetite. Therefore the will's object is naturally prior to its act: and consequently its first object precedes its every act. Therefore an
25 act of the will cannot be the first thing willed. But this is the last end, which is beatitude. Therefore beatitude or happiness cannot be the very act of the will.

Besides. In all those powers which are able to reflect on their acts, their act must first bear on some other object, and afterwards
30 the power is brought to bear on its own act. For if the intellect understand that it understands, we must suppose first that it understands some particular thing, and that afterwards it understands that it understands: for this very act of intelligence which the intellect understands, must have an object. Hence either
35 we must go on for ever, or if we come to some first thing understood, this will not be an act of understanding, but some intelligible thing. In the same way the first thing willed cannot be the very act of willing, but must be some other good. Now the first thing willed by an intelligent nature, is beatitude or
40 happiness: because for its sake we will whatever we will. Therefore happiness cannot consist in an act of the will.

Further. The truth of a thing's nature is derived from those things which constitute its essence: for a true man differs from a man in a picture, by the things which constitute man's essence. Now false happiness does not differ from true in an act of the will:
5 because whatever be proposed to the will as the supreme good, whether truly or falsely, it makes no difference to the will, desiring, loving, or enjoying that good: the difference is on the part of the intellect, as to whether the good proposed as supreme be truly so or not. Therefore beatitude or happiness consists
10 essentially in an act of the intellect rather than of the will.

Again. If an act of the will were happiness itself, this act would be either desire, or love, or joy. But desire cannot possibly be the last end. For desire implies that the will is tending to what it has not yet; and this is contrary to the very notion of the last
15 end. Nor can love be the last end. For a good is loved not only while it is in our possession, but even when it is not: because it is through love that we seek by desire what we have not: and if love of a thing we possess is more perfect, this arises from the fact that we possess the good we love. It is one thing, therefore, to possess
20 the good which is our end; and another to love it, which love before we possessed was imperfect, and perfect after we obtained possession. Nor again is delight the last end. For it is possession of the good that causes delight; whether we are conscious of possessing it actually; or call to mind our previous possession; or
25 hope to possess it in the future. Therefore delight is not the last end. Therefore no act of the will can be happiness itself essentially.

Furthermore. If delight were the last end, it would be desirable for its own sake. But this is not true. Because the
30 desirability of a delight depends on what gives rise to the delight: since that which arises from good and desirable operations, is itself good and desirable, but that which arises from evil operations, is itself evil and to be avoided. Therefore its goodness and desirability are from something else: and consequently it is not
35 itself the last end or happiness.

Moreover. The right order of things agrees with the order of nature: for in the natural order things are directed to their end without any error. Now, in the natural order delight is on account of operation and not conversely. For it is to be observed that
40 nature has joined delight with those animal operations which are clearly directed to necessary ends; for instance to the use of food that is directed to the preservation of the individual; and to sexual

matters, that are appointed for the preservation of the species: since were there no pleasure, animals would abstain from the use of these necessary things. Therefore delight cannot be the last end.

Again. Delight, seemingly, is nothing else than the quiescence
5 of the will in some becoming good, just as desire is the inclining of the will towards the attaining of some good. Now just as by his will, a man is inclined towards an end, and rests in it; so too have natural bodies a natural inclination to their respective ends, and are at rest when they have once attained their end. Now it is
10 absurd to say that the end of the movement of a heavy body is not to be in its proper place, but that it is the quiescence of the inclination towards that place. For if it were nature's chief intent that this inclination should be quiescent, it would not give such an inclination: but it gives it so that the body may tend towards its
15 place: and when it has arrived there, as though it were its end, quiescence of the inclination follows. Hence this quiescence is not the end, but accompanies the end. Neither therefore is delight the ultimate end, but accompanies it. Much less therefore is happiness any act of the will.

20   Besides. If a thing have something extrinsic for its end, the operation whereby it first obtains that thing will be called its last end: thus for those whose end is money, possession is said to be their end, but not love or desire. Now the last end of the intellective substance is God. Hence that operation of man
25 whereby he first obtains God is essentially his happiness or beatitude. And this is understanding: since we cannot will what we do not understand. Therefore man's ultimate happiness is essentially to know God by the intellect, and not an act of the will.

From what has been said we can now solve the arguments that
30 were objected in the contrary sense. For it does not necessarily follow that happiness is essentially the very act of the will, from the fact that it is the object of the will, through being the highest good, as the first argument reasoned. On the contrary the fact that it is the first object of the will, shows that it is not an act of the
35 will, as appears from what we have said.

Nor does it follow that whatever perfects a thing in any way whatever, must be the end of that thing; as the second objection argued. For a thing perfects another in two ways: first it perfects a thing that has its species; secondly it perfects a thing that it may
40 have its species. Thus the perfection of a house considered as already having its species, is that to which the species "house" is directed, namely to be a dwelling: for one would not build a house

but for that: and consequently we must include this in the definition of a house, if the definition is to be perfect. On the other hand the perfection that conduces to the species of a house, is both that which is directed to the completion of the species, for
5 instance its essential principles; and that which conduces to the preservation of the species, for instance the buttresses which are made to support the building; and those things which make the house more fit for use, for instance, the symmetry of the building. Accordingly that which is the perfection of a thing considered as
10 already having its species, is its end; as the end of a house is to be a dwelling. Likewise, the operation proper to a thing, its use, as it were, is its end. On the other hand whatever perfects a thing by conducing to its species, is not the end of that thing: in fact the thing is its end; thus matter and form are for the sake of the
15 species. For although the form is the end of generation, it is not the end of the thing already generated and having its species, but is required in order that the species be complete. Again, things that preserve the thing in its species, such as health and the nutritive power, although they perfect the animal, are not the animal's end,
20 but vice versa. And again, those things that adapt a thing for the perfection of its proper specific operations, and for the easier attainment of its proper end, are not the end of that thing, but vice versa: for instance, a man's comeliness and bodily strength, and the like, of which the Philosopher says (1 *Ethic.* viii., ix.) that they
25 conduce to happiness instrumentally. Now delight is a perfection of operation, not as though operation were directed thereto in respect of its species, for thus it is directed to other ends; thus eating, in respect of its species, is directed to the preservation of the individual: but it is like a perfection that is conducive to a
30 thing's species: since for the sake of the delight we perform more attentively and becomingly an operation we delight in. Wherefore the Philosopher (10 *Ethic.* iv.) says that delight perfects operation as beauty perfects youth: for beauty is for the sake of the one who has youth. Nor is the fact that men seek delight not for the sake of
35 something else but for its own sake, a sufficient indication that delight is the last end, as the third objection argued. Because delight, though it is not the last end, nevertheless accompanies the last end: since delight arises from the attainment of the end.

Nor do more people seek the pleasure that comes from
40 knowledge, than knowledge itself. But more there are who seek sensible delights than intellectual knowledge and the delight consequent thereto: because those things that are without, are

better known to the majority, in that human knowledge takes its beginning from sensible objects.

The suggestion put forward by the fifth argument, that the will is a higher power than the intellect, as being the latter's
5 motive force, is clearly untrue. Because the intellect moves the will, first and *per se*: for the will, as such, is moved by its object, which is the apprehended good: whereas the will moves the intellect accidentally as it were, in so far, to wit, that the act of intelligence is itself apprehended as a good, and on that account is
10 desired by the will, the result being that the intellect understands actually. Even in this, the intellect precedes the will, for the will would never seek the act of intelligence, did not the intellect first apprehend its act of intelligence as a good. And again, the will moves the intellect to actual operation, in the same way as an
15 agent is said to move; whereas the intellect moves the will in the same way as the end moves, for the good understood is the end of the will. Now the agent in moving comes after the end, for the agent does not move except on account of the end. It is therefore clear that the intellect is simply higher than the will; while the will
20 is higher than the intellect accidentally and in a restricted sense.

CHAPTER XXVII

25   THAT HUMAN HAPPINESS DOES NOT CONSIST
IN CARNAL PLEASURES

FROM what has been said it is clearly impossible that human happiness consist in pleasures of the body, the chief of which are
30 pleasures of the table and of sex.

It has been shown that according to nature's order, pleasure is on account of operation, and not conversely. Wherefore if an operation be not the ultimate end, the consequent pleasure can neither be the ultimate end, nor accompany the ultimate end.
35 Now it is manifest that the operations which are followed by the pleasures mentioned above, are not the last end: for they are directed to certain manifest ends; eating, for instance, to the preservation of the body, and carnal intercourse to the begetting of children. Therefore the aforesaid pleasures are not the last end,
40 nor do they accompany the last end. Therefore happiness does not consist in them.

Again. The will is higher than the sensitive appetite: for it moves it, as stated above. But happiness does not consist in an act of the will, as we have already proved. Much less therefore does it consist in the aforesaid pleasures which are seated in the sensitive
5 appetite.

Moreover. Happiness is a good proper to man: for it is an abuse of terms to speak of dumb animals as being happy. Now these pleasures are common to man and beast. Therefore we must not assign happiness to them.

10 Besides. The highest perfection of man cannot consist in his being united to things lower than himself, but consists in his being united to something above him; for the end is better than that which tends to the end. Now these pleasures consist in man being united through his senses to things beneath him, namely certain
15 sensible objects. Therefore we must not assign happiness to suchlike pleasures.

Further. That which is not good unless it be moderate, is not good in itself, but receives its goodness from its moderator. Now the use of the aforesaid pleasures is not good for man unless it be
20 moderate: for otherwise they would frustrate one another. Therefore these pleasures are not in themselves man's good. But the sovereign good is good essentially, because that which is good of itself is better than what is good through another. Therefore suchlike pleasures are not man's supreme good, which is
25 happiness.

Again. In all *per se* predications, if A be predicated of B simply, an increase in A will be predicated of an increase in B: thus if a hot thing heats, a hotter thing heats more, and the hottest thing heats most. Accordingly if the pleasures in question were good in
30 themselves, it would follow that to use them very much is very good. But this is clearly false: because it is considered sinful to use them too much: besides it is hurtful to the body, and hinders pleasures of the same kind. Therefore they are not *per se* man's good: and human happiness does not consist in them.

35 Again. Acts of virtue are praiseworthy through being directed to happiness. If therefore human happiness consisted in the aforesaid pleasures, an act of virtue would be more praiseworthy in acceding to them than in abstaining from them. But this is clearly untrue: for the act of temperance is especially praised in
40 abstinence from pleasures; whence that act takes its name. Therefore man's happiness is not in these pleasures.

Furthermore. The last end of everything is God, as was proved above. We must therefore posit as man's last end that by which especially man approaches to God. Now man is hindered by the aforesaid pleasures from his chief approach to God, which is
5 effected by contemplation, to which these same pleasures are a very great hindrance, since more than anything they plunge man into the midst of sensible things, and consequently withdraw him from intelligible things. Therefore human happiness is not to be placed in bodily pleasures.

10 Hereby is refuted the error of the Epicureans who ascribed man's happiness to pleasures of this kind: in their person Solomon says (Eccles. v. 17): This therefore hath seemed good to me, that a man should eat and drink, and enjoy the fruit of his labour . . . and this is his portion: and (Wis. ii. 9): Let us everywhere leave tokens
15 of joy: for this is our portion, and this is our lot.

The error of the Cerinthians is also refuted: for they pretended that, in the state of final happiness, after the resurrection Christ will reign for a thousand years, and men will indulge in the carnal pleasures of the table: wherefore they are
20 called 'Chiliastae,' or believers in the Millennium.

The fables of the Jews and Mohammedans are also refuted: who pretend that the reward of the righteous consists in suchlike pleasures: for happiness is the reward of virtue.

25

CHAPTER XXVIII

THAT HAPPINESS DOES NOT CONSIST IN HONOURS

30 FROM the foregoing it is also clear that neither does man's supreme good, or happiness, consist in honours.

For man's ultimate end and happiness is his most perfect operation, as we have shown above. But man's honour does not consist in something done by him, but in something done to him
35 by another who shows him honour. Therefore man's happiness must not be placed in honours.

Again. That which is on account of another good and desirable thing is not the last end. Now such is honour: for a man is not rightly honoured, except on account of some other good in him.
40 For this reason do men seek to be honoured, as though wishing to have a voucher for some good that is in them: so that they rejoice

more in being honoured by the great and the wise. Therefore we must not assign man's happiness to honours.

Besides. Happiness is obtained through virtue. Now virtuous deeds are voluntary, else they were not praiseworthy. Therefore
5 happiness must be a good obtainable by man through his will. But it is not in a man's power to secure honour, rather is it in the power of the man who pays honour. Therefore happiness is not to be assigned to honours.

Moreover. Only the good can be worthy of honour: and yet it
10 is possible even for the wicked to be honoured. Therefore it is better to become worthy of honour, than to be honoured. Therefore honour is not man's supreme good.

Furthermore. The supreme good is the perfect good. Now the perfect good is incompatible with any evil. But that which has no
15 evil in it cannot possibly be evil. Therefore that which is in possession of the supreme good cannot be evil. Yet it is possible for an evil person to receive honour. Therefore honour is not man's supreme good.

20

CHAPTER XXIX

THAT MAN'S HAPPINESS CONSISTS NOT IN GLORY

25   WHEREFORE it is evident also that man's supreme good does not consist in glory which is the recognition of one's good name.

For glory, according to Cicero, is the general recognition and praise of a person's good name, and in the words of Ambrose
30 consists in being well known and praised. Now men seek praise and distinction through being famous, so that they may be honoured by those whom their fame reaches. Therefore glory is sought for the sake of honour: and consequently if honour be not the sovereign good, much less is glory.

35   Again. Those goods are worthy of praise, whereby a man shows himself to be directed to his end. Now he who is directed to his end has not yet reached his last end. Therefore praise is not bestowed on one who has reached his last end: rather does he receive honour as the Philosopher says (1 *Ethic.* xii.). Therefore
40 glory cannot be the supreme good: since it consists chiefly in praise.

Besides. It is better to know than to be known: because only the higher things know; whereas the lowest are known. Therefore man's supreme good cannot be glory, which consists in a man being known.

5 Further. A man does not seek to be known except in good things: and in evil things he seeks to be hidden. Therefore to be known is good and desirable, on account of the good things that are known in a man. Therefore these good things are better still. Consequently glory, which consists in a man being known, is not 10 his supreme good.

Moreover. The supreme good must needs be perfect, for it satisfies the appetite. But the knowledge of one's good name, wherein glory consists, is imperfect: for it is beset with much uncertainty and error. Therefore glory of this kind cannot be the 15 supreme good.

Furthermore. Man's supreme good must be supremely stable in human things: for it is natural to desire unfailing endurance in one's goods. Now glory, which consists in fame, is most unstable; since nothing is more changeable than human opinion and praise. 20 Therefore such glory is not man's supreme good.

CHAPTER XXX

25 THAT MAN'S HAPPINESS DOES NOT CONSIST IN WEALTH

HENCE it is evident that neither is wealth man's supreme good. For wealth is not sought except for the sake of something else: because of itself it brings us no good, but only when we use 30 it, whether for the support of the body, or for some similar purpose. Now the supreme good is sought for its own, and not for another's sake. Therefore wealth is not man's supreme good.

Again. Man's supreme good cannot consist in the possession or preservation of things whose chief advantage for man consists in 35 their being spent. Now the chief advantage of wealth is in its being spent; for this is its use. Therefore the possession of wealth cannot be man's supreme good.

Moreover. Acts of virtue deserve praise according as they lead to happiness. Now acts of liberality and magnificence which are 40 concerned with money, are deserving of praise, on account of money being spent, rather than on account of its being kept: and it is from this that these virtues derive their names. Therefore man's happiness does not consist in the possession of wealth.

Besides. Man's supreme good must consist in obtaining something better than man. But man is better than wealth: since it 5 is something directed to man's use. Therefore not in wealth does man's supreme good consist.

Further. Man's supreme good is not subject to chance. For things that happen by chance, escape the forethought of reason: whereas man has to attain his own end by means of his reason. But 10 chance occupies the greater place in the attaining of wealth. Therefore human happiness consists not in wealth.

Moreover. This is evident from the fact that wealth is lost unwillingly. Also because wealth can come into the possession of evil persons, who, of necessity, must lack the sovereign good. 15 Again because wealth is unstable. Other similar reasons can be gathered from the arguments given above.

CHAPTER XXXI

20

THAT HAPPINESS CONSISTS NOT IN WORLDLY POWER

IN like manner neither can worldly power be man's supreme happiness: since in the achievement thereof chance can effect 25 much. Again it is unstable; and is not subject to man's will; and is often obtained by evil men. These are incompatible with the supreme good, as already stated.

Again. Man is said to be good especially according as he approaches the supreme good. But in respect to his having power, 30 he is not said to be either good or evil: since not everyone who can do good deeds is good, nor is a person evil because he can do evil deeds. Therefore the supreme good does not consist in being powerful.

Besides. Every power implies reference to something else. 35 But the supreme good is not referred to anything further. Therefore power is not man's supreme good.

Moreover. Man's supreme good cannot be a thing that one can use both well and ill: for the better things are those that we cannot abuse. But one can use one's power both well and ill: for 40 rational powers can be directed to contrary objects. Therefore human power is not man's supreme good.

Further. If any power be man's supreme good, it must be most perfect. Now human power is most imperfect: for it is based on human will and opinion, which are full of inconsistencies. Also the greater a power is reputed to be, the greater number of people
5 does it depend on: which again conduces to its weakness, since what depends on many, is in many ways destructible. Therefore man's supreme good does not consist in worldly power. Consequently man's happiness consists in no external good: for all external goods, which are known as goods of chance, are
10 contained under those we have mentioned.

CHAPTER XXXII

15   THAT HAPPINESS CONSISTS NOT IN GOODS OF THE BODY

LIKE arguments avail to prove that man's supreme good does not consist in goods of the body, such as health, beauty and strength. For they are common to good and evil: and are unstable:
20 and are not subject to the will.

Besides. The soul is better than the body, which neither lives, nor possesses these goods, without the soul. Wherefore the soul's good, such as understanding and the like, is better than the body's good. Therefore the body's good is not man's supreme good.
25   Again. These goods are common to man and other animals: whereas happiness is a good proper to man. Therefore man's happiness does not consist in the things mentioned.

Moreover. Many animals surpass man in goods of the body: for some are fleeter than he, some more sturdy, and so on.
30 Accordingly, if man's supreme good consisted in these things, man would not excel all animals: which is clearly untrue. Therefore human happiness does not consist in goods of the body.

CHAPTER XXXIII

35

THAT HUMAN HAPPINESS IS NOT SEATED IN THE SENSES

BY the same arguments it is evident that neither does man's
40 supreme good consist in goods of his sensitive faculty. For these goods again, are common to man and other animals.

Again. Intellect is superior to sense. Therefore the intellect's good is better than the sense's. Consequently man's supreme good is not seated in the senses.

Besides. The greatest sensual pleasures are those of the table
5 and of sex, wherein the supreme good must needs be, if seated in the senses. But it does not consist in them. Therefore man's supreme good is not in the senses.

Moreover. The senses are appreciated for their utility and for knowledge. Now the entire utility of the senses is referred to the
10 goods of the body. Again, sensitive knowledge is directed to intellective: wherefore animals devoid of intelligence take no pleasure in sensation except in reference to some bodily utility, in so far as by sensitive knowledge they obtain food or sexual intercourse. Therefore man's supreme good which is happiness is
15 not seated in the sensitive faculty.

CHAPTER XXXIV

20 THAT MAN'S ULTIMATE HAPPINESS DOES NOT CONSIST IN ACTS OF MORAL VIRTUE

IT is clear that man's ultimate happiness does not consist in moral works.

25 For human happiness, if ultimate, cannot be directed to a further end. But all moral deeds can be directed to something else. This is clear from a consideration of the principal among them. Because deeds of fortitude in time of war are directed to victory and peace: for it were foolish to go to war merely for its own
30 sake. Again deeds of justice are directed to keeping peace among men, through each one possessing his own in peace. The same applies to all other virtues. Therefore man's ultimate happiness is not in moral deeds.

Again. The purpose of the moral virtues is that through them
35 we may observe the mean in the passions within us, and in things outside us. Now it is impossible that the moderation of passions or of external things be the ultimate end of man's life; since both passions and external things can be directed to something less. Therefore it is not possible that the practice of moral virtue be
40 man's final happiness.

Further. Since man is man through having reason, his proper good which is happiness must needs be in accordance with that

which is proper to reason. Now that which reason has in itself is more proper to reason than what it effects in something else. Seeing then that the good of moral virtue is something effected by reason in something other than itself, it cannot be man's greatest
5 good which is happiness: rather must it be a good that is in reason itself.

Moreover. We have already proved that the last end of all is to become like God. Therefore that in which man chiefly becomes like God, is his happiness. Now this is not in regard to moral
10 actions, since suchlike actions cannot be ascribed to God, except metaphorically; for it is not becoming to God to have passions, or the like, with which moral virtue is concerned. Therefore man's ultimate happiness, which is his last end, does not consist in moral actions.

15 Furthermore. Happiness is man's proper good. Therefore that good, which of all goods is most proper to man in comparison with other animals, is the one in which we must seek his ultimate happiness. Now this is not the practice of moral virtue; for animals share somewhat either in liberality, or in fortitude: whereas no
20 animal has a share in intellectual action. Therefore man's ultimate happiness does not consist in moral actions.

CHAPTER XXXV

25

THAT ULTIMATE HAPPINESS DOES NOT CONSIST IN THE ACT OF PRUDENCE

IT is also evident from the foregoing that neither does man's
30 happiness consist in the act of prudence.

For acts of prudence are solely about matters of moral virtue. But human happiness does not consist in the practice of moral virtue. Neither therefore does it consist in the practice of prudence.

35 Again. Man's ultimate happiness consists in man's most excellent operation. Now man's most excellent operation in respect of what is proper to man, is in relation to most perfect objects. But the act of prudence is not concerned with the most perfect objects of intellect or reason: since it is not about
40 necessary things, but about contingent practical matters. Therefore its act is not man's ultimate happiness.

Besides. That which is directed to another as its end, is not man's ultimate happiness. Now the act of prudence is directed to another as its end: both because all practical knowledge, under which prudence is comprised, is directed to operation: and 5 because prudence gives man a good disposition as regards things directed to the end, as may be gathered from Aristotle (6 Ethic. xiii.). Therefore man's ultimate happiness is not in the practice of prudence.

Furthermore. Irrational animals have no share of happiness: as 10 Aristotle proves (1 *Ethic*. ix.). Yet some of them have a certain share of prudence: as may be gathered from the same authority (1 *Metaph*. i., ii.). Therefore happiness does not consist in an act of prudence.

15

CHAPTER XXXVI

THAT HAPPINESS DOES NOT CONSIST IN THE PRACTICE OF ART

20
IT is also evident that it cannot consist in the practice of art.

For even the knowledge of art is practical, and so is directed to an end, and is not the ultimate end.

Besides. The end of the practice of art is the thing produced 25 by art: and such a thing cannot be the ultimate end of human life; since rather is it we who are the end of those products, for they are all made for man's use. Therefore final happiness cannot consist in the practice of art.

30

CHAPTER XXXVII

THAT MAN'S ULTIMATE HAPPINESS CONSISTS IN CONTEMPLATING GOD

35
ACCORDINGLY if man's ultimate happiness consists not in external things, which are called goods of chance; nor in goods of the body; nor in goods of the soul, as regards the sensitive faculty; nor as regards the intellective faculty, in the practice of moral 40 virtue; nor as regards intellectual virtue in those which are concerned about action, namely art and prudence; it remains for

us to conclude that man's ultimate happiness consists in the contemplation of the truth.

For this operation alone is proper to man, and none of the other animals communicates with him therein.

5   Again. This is not directed to anything further as its end: since the contemplation of the truth is sought for its own sake.

Again. By this operation man is united to things above him, by becoming like them: because of all human actions this alone is both in God and in separate substances. Also, by this operation
10 man comes into contact with those higher beings, through knowing them in any way whatever.

Besides, man is more self-sufficing for this operation, seeing that he stands in little need of the help of external things in order to perform it.

15 Further. All other human operations seem to be directed to this as their end. Because perfect contemplation requires that the body should be disencumbered, and to this effect are directed all the products of art that are necessary for life. Moreover, it requires freedom from the disturbance caused by the passions,
20 which is achieved by means of the moral virtues and prudence; and freedom from external disturbance, to which all the regulations of the civil life are directed. So that, if we consider the matter rightly, we shall see that all human occupations are brought into the service of those who contemplate the truth. Now, it is not
25 possible that man's ultimate happiness consist in contemplation based on the understanding of first principles: for this is most imperfect, as being universal and containing potential knowledge of things. Moreover, it is the beginning and not the end of human study, and comes to us from nature, and not through the study of
30 the truth. Nor does it consist in contemplation based on the sciences that have the lowest things for their object: since happiness must consist in an operation of the intellect in relation to the highest objects of intelligence. It follows then that man's ultimate happiness consists in wisdom, based on the consideration
35 of divine things. It is therefore evident by way of induction that man's ultimate happiness consists solely in the contemplation of God, which conclusion was proved above by arguments.

CHAPTER XXXVIII

THAT HUMAN HAPPINESS DOES NOT CONSIST
IN THE KNOWLEDGE OF GOD WHICH IS
5   POSSESSED GENERALLY BY THE MAJORITY

IT remains for us to inquire in what kind of knowledge of God
the ultimate happiness of the intellectual substance consists. For
there is a certain general and confused knowledge of God, which is
10 in almost all men, whether from the fact that, as some think, the
existence of God, like other principles of demonstration, is self-
evident, as we have stated in the First Book: or, as seems nearer to
the truth, because by his natural reason, man is able at once to
arrive at some knowledge of God. For seeing that natural things
15 are arranged in a certain order,—since there cannot be order
without a cause of order—men, for the most part, perceive that
there is one who arranges in order the things that we see. But who
or of what kind this cause of order may be, or whether there be
but one, cannot be gathered from this general consideration: even
20 so, when we see a man in motion, and performing other works,
we perceive that in him there is a cause of these operations, which
is not in other things, and we give this cause the name of soul, but
without knowing yet what the soul is, whether it be a body, or
how it brings about operations in question.

25   Now, this knowledge of God cannot possibly suffice for
happiness.

For the operation of the happy must be without any defect:
and this knowledge is subject to an admixture of many errors.
Some believed that there is no other ordainer of mundane things
30 than the heavenly bodies; wherefore they said that the heavenly
bodies are gods. Some ascribed this order to the elements and to
the things generated from them; as though they deemed the
movements and natural operations thereof, not to be due to
another ordainer, and the order in other things to be caused by
35 them. Some, deeming human acts not to be subject to any but a
human ordinance, declared that men who cause order in other
men are gods. Accordingly this knowledge of God is not sufficient
for happiness.

Moreover. Happiness is the end of human acts. But human
40 acts are not directed to the aforesaid knowledge as their end:
indeed, it is in everyone almost from the very beginning.

Therefore happiness does not consist in this kind of knowledge of God.

Again. No one appears to be blamed for lacking happiness: nay, those who have it not and seek it are praised. Whereas he
5 who lacks the aforesaid knowledge of God, is seemingly very much to be blamed: since it is a very clear sign of a man's dullness of perception, if he fail to perceive such evident signs of God's existence: even as a man would be deemed dull who, seeing man, understood not that he has a soul. Hence it is said in the Psalm
10 (xiii. 1: lii. 1): The fool hath said in his heart: There is no God.

Further. Knowledge of a thing in general only, and not in respect of a property thereof, is most imperfect; for instance knowledge of man from the fact that he is moved, for this is a knowledge whereby a thing is known only potentially: because the
15 proper is only potentially contained in the common. Now happiness is a perfect operation: and man's supreme good must needs be in respect of what he is actually, and not in respect of what he only potentially: since potentiality perfected by act has the aspect of a good. Therefore the aforesaid knowledge of God is
20 not sufficient for our happiness.

CHAPTER XXXIX

25   THAT MAN'S HAPPINESS DOES NOT CONSIST IN THE
KNOWLEDGE OF GOD ACQUIRED BY DEMONSTRATION

THERE is also another knowledge of God, higher than the one just mentioned, which is acquired by means of a demonstration, and
30 which approaches nearer to a proper knowledge of him: since by means of a demonstration many things are removed from him, so that in consequence we understand him as something apart from other things. For demonstration proves that God is immovable, eternal, incorporeal, utterly simple, one, and the like, as we have
35 shown in the First Book. Now we arrive at the proper knowledge of a thing not only by affirmation, but also by negation: for just as it is proper to man to be a rational animal, so is it proper to him not to be inanimate or irrational. Yet there is this difference between these two modes of knowledge, that when we have
40 proper knowledge of a thing by affirmation, we know what that thing is, and how it is distinguished from others: whereas when we have proper knowledge of a thing by negations, we know that it is

distinct from others, but remain ignorant of what it is. Such is the proper knowledge of God, that can be obtained by demonstrations. But neither does this suffice for man's ultimate happiness. For things belonging to one species for the most part
5 attain to the end of that species, because nature achieves its purpose always or nearly always, and fails in a few instances on account of some corruption. Now happiness is the end of the human species; since all men naturally desire it. Therefore happiness is a common good that can be attained by all men,
10 unless some obstacle occur to some whereby they be debarred from it. Few, however, attain to the possession of the aforesaid knowledge of God by way of demonstration, on account of the obstacles to this knowledge, mentioned at the beginning of this work. Therefore this knowledge is not essentially man's
15 happiness.

Again. Actual existence is the end of that which exists potentially, as was made clear above. Wherefore happiness that is the last end, is an act free of any potentiality to a further act. Now this knowledge of God that is acquired by way of demonstration is
20 still in potentiality to a further knowledge of God, or to the same knowledge, but by a better way: because those who came afterwards endeavoured to add something to the knowledge of God besides that which they found handed down to them by those who preceded them. Therefore such knowledge is not man's
25 ultimate happiness.

Further. Happiness excludes all unhappiness: for no man can be at the same time happy and unhappy. Now deception and error have a large place in unhappiness, since all naturally avoid them. But the aforesaid knowledge of God is subject to the admixture of
30 many errors: as evidenced by many who knew some truths about God through demonstration, yet, following their own opinions, when they lacked proof, fell into many errors. And if some there were who by the way of demonstration discovered the truth about divine things, without any admixture of error in their opinions, it
35 is evident that they were very few: which is inconsistent with happiness which should be the common end. Therefore man's ultimate happiness is not seated in such knowledge as this.

Moreover. Happiness consists in a perfect operation. Now perfect knowledge requires certitude: hence we cannot be said to
40 know, unless we be certain that it cannot be otherwise, as stated in 1 Poster. ii. But the aforesaid knowledge is beset with uncertainty: as evidenced by the diversity of sciences about divine

things, elaborated by those who endeavoured to discover something about them by the way of demonstration. Therefore ultimate happiness does not consist in suchlike knowledge.

Besides. When the will has obtained its last end, its desire is at
5 rest. Now the ultimate end of all human knowledge is happiness. Therefore happiness is essentially that knowledge of God the possession of which leaves no knowledge to be desired of anything knowable. Such, however, is not the knowledge which philosophers were able to have about God by the way of
10 demonstration: because even when we have that knowledge we still desire to know something more;—things that we know not by means of the aforesaid knowledge. Therefore happiness does not consist in suchlike knowledge of God.

Furthermore. The end of everything that is in potentiality is
15 that it be brought to actuality: for to this does it tend by means of the movement with which it is moved to its end. Now everything that is in potentiality tends to be actualized as far as possible. For there are things in potentiality in that their whole potentiality is reducible to act: so that the end of such a thing is that its whole
20 potentiality be actualized: thus a heavy body, that is outside its medium, is in potentiality to its proper place. There are also things whose potentiality cannot be actualized all at once,—for instance primary matter: so that by its movement it is appetent of actualization by various forms in succession, which cannot be in
25 matter at the same time on account of their diversity. Now our intellect is in potentiality to all things intelligible, as stated in the Second Book. And it is possible for two intelligible objects to be in the possible intellect at the same time in respect of the first act which is science: although perhaps not in respect of the second act
30 which is consideration. Accordingly it is clear that the whole potentiality of the possible intellect can be actualized at one time: and consequently this is required for its ultimate end which is happiness. But the aforesaid knowledge which can be acquired about God by the way of demonstration, does not effect this: since
35 when we have it we still are ignorant of many things. Therefore suchlike knowledge of God does not suffice for ultimate happiness.

CHAPTER XL

THAT MAN'S HAPPINESS DOES NOT CONSIST IN THE KNOWLEDGE OF GOD BY FAITH

5 THERE is yet another knowledge of God, in one respect superior to the knowledge we have been discussing, namely that whereby God is known by men through faith. In this respect it surpasses the knowledge of God through demonstration, because by faith we
10 know certain things about God, which are so sublime that reason cannot reach them by means of demonstration, as we have stated at the beginning of this work. But not even in this knowledge of God can man's ultimate happiness consist.

For happiness is the intellect's perfect operation, as already
15 declared. But in knowledge by faith the operation of the intellect is found to be most imperfect as regards that which is on the part of the intellect:—although it is most perfect on the part of the object:—for the intellect in believing does not grasp the object of its assent. Therefore neither does man's happiness consist in this
20 knowledge of God.

Again. It has been shown that ultimate happiness does not consist chiefly in an act of the will. Now in knowledge by faith the will has the leading place: for the intellect assents by faith to things proposed to it, because it wills, and not through being constrained
25 by the evidence of their truth. Therefore man's final happiness does not consist in this knowledge.

Besides. The believer assents to things proposed to him by another, but not seen by himself: so that the knowledge of faith resembles hearing rather than seeing. Now a man does not believe
30 in what is unseen by him, and proposed to him by another, unless he thinks this other to have a more perfect knowledge of the things proposed, than he himself has who sees not. Either therefore the believer thinks wrong: or the proposer must have more perfect knowledge of the things proposed. And if the latter also knows
35 these things only through hearing them from another, we cannot proceed thus indefinitely: for then the assent of faith would be without foundation or certitude; since we should not come to some first principle certain in itself, to give certitude to the faith of believers. But it is not possible that the assent of faith be false
40 and without foundation, as is clear from what we have said at the beginning of this work: and yet if it were false and baseless, happiness could not consist in suchlike knowledge. There is

therefore some knowledge of God that is higher than the knowledge of faith: whether he who proposes faith sees the truth immediately, as when we believe Christ: or receive the truth from him who sees it immediately, as when we believe the Apostles and
5   prophets. Since then man's happiness consists in the highest knowledge of God, it cannot consist in the knowledge of faith.

Moreover. Since happiness is the last end, the natural desire is set at rest thereby. But the knowledge of faith does not set the desire at rest, but inflames it: because everyone desires to see
10   what he believes. Therefore man's ultimate happiness does not consist in the knowledge of faith.

Further. Knowledge of God has been declared to be the end, inasmuch as it unites us to the last end of all, namely God. Now the knowledge of faith does not make the thing believed to be
15   perfectly present to the mind: since faith is of distant, and not present things. Wherefore the Apostle says (2 Cor. v. 6, 7) that so long as we walk by faith, we are pilgrims from the Lord. Yet faith makes God to be present to the heart, since the believer assents to God voluntarily, according to the saying of Ephes. iii. 17: That
20   Christ may dwell by faith in our hearts. Therefore the knowledge of faith cannot be man's ultimate happiness.

*   *   *

25   ## CHAPTER XLVII

THAT IN THIS LIFE WE ARE UNABLE
TO SEE GOD IN HIS ESSENCE

30   IF, in this life, we are unable to understand separate substances by reason of our intellect's innate relation to phantasms, much less can we see the divine essence in this life, since it is far above all separate substances. We may take it as a sign of this, that the more our mind is raised to the contemplation
35   of spiritual things, the more is it withdrawn from sensible things. Now the divine substance is the highest term to which contemplation can reach: hence the mind that sees the divine substance must be wholly freed from the senses, either by death or by rapture. Wherefore it is said in God's person (Exod. xxxiii.
40   20): Man shall not see me, and live.

If it is stated in Holy Writ that some have seen God, we must understand this to have been either through an imaginary vision—

or even a bodily vision, the presence of the divine power being shown by corporeal species whether appearing externally, or formed internally in the imagination:—or by gathering some intellectual knowledge of God from His spiritual effects.

5   A difficulty, however, arises through some words of Augustine which would seem to imply that we are able to understand God in this life. For he says (9 De Trin. vii.) that with the eyes of the soul we see the form of our being and of our actions—whether effected in ourselves or truly and rightly on

10 other bodies—in the eternal truth, from which all temporal things proceed. Again (12 Conf. xxv.) he says: If we both see that what you say is true, and that what I say is true: where, I ask, do we see this? Surely, neither I in thee, nor thou in me; but both of us in the immutable truth itself which transcends our minds. And (De Vera

15 Relig. xxxi.) he says that we judge of all things according to the divine truth: and again (1. Solil. xv.): We must first know the truth by which other things can be known, referring, it would seem, to the divine truth. It would seem then, from his words, that we see God Himself who is His own truth, and that through

20 Him we know other things.

Other words of his would seem to point to the same conclusion, in 12 De Trin. ii., where he says: It is the duty of reason to judge of these corporeal things, according to the incorporeal and eternal ideas which, unless they were above the

25 human mind, would surely not be unchangeable. Now unchangeable and eternal ideas cannot be elsewhere than in God, since according to the teaching of faith, God alone is eternal. Accordingly it would seem to follow that we can see God in this life, and that through seeing Him and the ideas of things in Him,

30 we judge of other things.

Yet it is not to be believed that Augustine, by these words, meant that we are able in this life to see God in His essence. We must therefore inquire how, in this life, we see that unchangeable truth, or these eternal ideas, and how judge of them according to

35 it.

Augustine allows that truth is in the soul (2 Solil. xix.): wherefore he proves the immortality of the soul from the eternity of truth. Now truth is in the soul not only in the same way as God is said to be in all things by His essence; or as He is in all things by

40 His likeness,—a thing being true so far as it is like to God—for then the soul would not be higher than other things in this respect. It is therefore in the soul in a special way, forasmuch as the soul

knows the truth. Accordingly just as the soul and other things are said to be true in their nature, according as they are likened to that supreme nature, which is truth itself; since it is its own being understood by itself; so too, that which is known by the soul, is
5   true so far as it bears a likeness to that divine truth which God knows. Wherefore a gloss on Ps. xi. 2, Truths are decayed from among the children of men, says that as a mirror gives many reflections of one face, so are many truths reflected in men's minds from the first truth [Augustine, Enarr. in Ps. xi.]. Now
10   although different things are known, and different things believed to be true, by different people, yet some truths there are in which all men agree, such as first principles both of the speculative and of the practical intellect: inasmuch as a kind of image of the divine truth is reflected in the minds of all men.

15   Consequently when a mind knows with certitude anything at all, and by tracing it back to the principles by which we judge of everything, comes to see it in those principles, it is said to see all such things in the divine truth or in the eternal ideas, and to judge of all things according to them. This explanation is confirmed by
20   Augustine's words (1 Solil. viii.): The speculations of science are seen in the divine truth, even as these visible things are seen in the light of the sun: for it is evident that these things are not seen in the body of the sun, but by the light, which is a likeness of the solar brilliance reflected in the air, and cast upon such bodies.
25   Therefore, from these words of Augustine, we cannot conclude that God is seen in His essence in this life, but only as in a mirror: and to this the Apostle witnesses as regards the knowledge of this life (1 Cor. xiii. 12): We see now through a glass in a dark manner.

30   And though this mirror, which is the human mind, reflects the likeness of God more faithfully than creatures of lower degree, yet the knowledge of God that can be gathered from the human mind, does not surpass the knowledge gathered from sensible things: since even the soul knows what itself is through understanding the
35   nature of sensible things, as already stated [Ch. xlv., xlvi.]. Consequently even in this way God is not known in higher fashion than the cause is known from its effect.

CHAPTER XLVIII

THAT MAN'S ULTIMATE HAPPINESS IS NOT IN THIS LIFE

5   SEEING then that man's ultimate happiness does not consist
in that knowledge of God whereby he is known by all or many in a
vague kind of opinion, nor again in that knowledge of God
whereby he is known in science through demonstration, nor in
10 that knowledge whereby he is known through faith, as we have
proved above: and seeing that it is not possible in this life to arrive
at a higher knowledge of God in His essence, or at least so that we
understand other separate substances, and thus know God through
that which is nearest to Him, so to say, as we have proved; and
15 since we must place our ultimate happiness in some kind of
knowledge of God, as we have shown; it is impossible for man's
happiness to be in this life.

Again. Man's last end is the term of his natural appetite, so
that when he has obtained it, he desires nothing more: because if
20 he still has a movement towards something, he has not yet reached
an end wherein to be at rest. Now, this cannot happen in this life:
since the more man understands, the more is the desire to
understand increased in him,—this being natural to man,—unless
perhaps someone there be who understands all things: and in this
25 life this never did nor can happen to anyone that was a mere man;
seeing that in this life we are unable to know separate substances
which in themselves are most intelligible, as we have proved.
Therefore man's ultimate happiness cannot possibly be in this life.

Besides. Whatever is in motion towards an end, has a natural
30 desire to be established and at rest therein: hence a body does not
move away from the place towards which it has a natural
movement, except by a violent movement which is contrary to
that appetite. Now happiness is the last end which man desires
naturally. Therefore it is his natural desire to be established in
35 happiness. Consequently unless together with happiness he
acquires a state of immobility, he is not yet happy, since his natural
desire is not yet at rest. When therefore a man acquires happiness,
he also acquires stability and rest; so that all agree in conceiving
stability as a necessary condition of happiness: hence the
40 Philosopher says (1 *Ethic*. x.): We do not look upon the happy
man as a kind of chameleon. Now, in this life there is no sure
stability; since, however happy a man may be, sickness and

misfortune may come upon him, so that he is hindered in the operation, whatever it be, in which his happiness consists. Therefore man's ultimate happiness cannot be in this life.

Moreover. It would seem unfitting and unreasonable for a
5   thing to take a long time in becoming, and to have but a short time in being: for it would follow that for a longer duration of time nature would be deprived of its end; hence we see that animals which live but a short time, are perfected in a short time. But, if happiness consists in a perfect operation according to perfect
10   virtue. whether intellectual or moral, it cannot possibly come to man except after a long time. This is most evident in speculative matters, wherein man's ultimate happiness consists, as we have proved: for hardly is man able to arrive at perfection in the speculations of science, even though he reach the last stage of life:
15   and then in the majority of cases, but a short space of life remains to him. Therefore man's ultimate happiness cannot be in this life.

Further. All admit that happiness is a perfect good: else it would not bring rest to the appetite. Now perfect good is that which is wholly free from any admixture of evil: just as that which
20   is perfectly white is that which is entirely free from any admixture of black. But man cannot be wholly free from evils in this state of life; not only from evils of the body, such as hunger, thirst, heat, cold and the like, but also from evils of the soul. For no one is there who at times is not disturbed by inordinate passions; who
25   sometimes does not go beyond the mean, wherein virtue consists, either in excess or in deficiency; who is not deceived in some thing or another; or at least ignores what he would wish to know, or feels doubtful about an opinion of which he would like to be certain. Therefore no man is happy in this life.

30   Again. Man naturally shuns death, and is sad about it: not only shunning it now when he feels its presence, but also when he thinks about it. But man, in this life, cannot obtain not to die. Therefore it is not possible for man to be happy in this life.

Besides. Ultimate happiness consists not in a habit but in an
35   operation: since habits are for the sake of actions. But in this life it is impossible to perform any action continuously. Therefore man cannot be entirely happy in this life.

Further. The more a thing is desired and loved, the more does its loss bring sorrow and pain. Now happiness is most desired and
40   loved. Therefore its loss brings the greatest sorrow. But if there be ultimate happiness in this life, it will certainly be lost, at least by death. Nor is it certain that it will last till death: since it is possible

for every man in this life to encounter sickness, whereby he is wholly hindered from the operation of virtue; such as madness and the like which hinder the use of reason. Such happiness therefore always has sorrow naturally connected with it: and consequently it
5 will not be perfect happiness.

But someone might say that, since happiness is a good of the intellectual nature, perfect and true happiness is for those in whom the intellectual nature is perfect, namely in separate substances: and that it is imperfect in man, by way of a kind of
10 participation. Because he can arrive at a full understanding of the truth, only by a sort of movement of inquiry; and fails entirely to understand things that are by nature most intelligible, as we have proved.   Wherefore neither is happiness, in its perfect form, possible to man: yet he has a certain participation thereof, even in
15 this life. This seems to have been Aristotle's opinion about happiness. Wherefore (1 *Ethic.* x.) inquiring whether misfortunes destroy happiness, he shows that happiness seems especially to consist in deeds of virtue, which seem to be most stable in this life, and concludes that those who in this life attain to this perfection,
20 are happy as men, as though not attaining to happiness simply, but in a human way.

We must now show that this explanation does not avoid the foregoing arguments. For although man is below the separate substances in the natural order, he is above irrational creatures:
25 wherefore he attains his ultimate end in a more perfect way than they. Now these attain their last end so perfectly that they seek nothing further: thus a heavy body rests when it is in its own proper place; and when an animal enjoys sensible pleasure, its natural desire is at rest. Much more therefore when man has
30 obtained his last end, must his natural desire be at rest. But this cannot happen in this life. Therefore in this life man does not obtain happiness considered as his proper end, as we have proved. Therefore he must obtain it after this life.

Again. The natural desire cannot be void; since nature does
35 nothing in vain. But nature's desire would be void if it could never be fulfilled. Therefore man's natural desire can be fulfilled. But not in this life, as we have shown. Therefore it must be fulfilled after this life. Therefore man's ultimate happiness is after this life.

Besides. As long as a thing is in motion towards perfection it
40 has not reached its last end. Now in the knowledge of truth all men are ever in motion and tending towards perfection: because those who follow, make discoveries in addition to those made by

their predecessors, as stated in 2 *Metaph.* Therefore in the knowledge of truth man is not situated as though he had arrived at his last end. Since then as Aristotle himself shows (10 *Ethic.* vii.) man's ultimate happiness in this life consists apparently in
5 speculation, whereby he seeks the knowledge of truth, we cannot possibly allow that man obtains his last end in this life.

Moreover. Whatever is in potentiality tends to become actual: so that as long as it is not wholly actual, it has not reached its last end. Now our intellect is in potentiality to the knowledge
10 of the forms of all things: and it becomes actual when it knows any one of them. Consequently it will not be wholly actual, nor in possession of its last end, except when it knows all, at least these material things. But man cannot obtain this through speculative sciences, by which in this life we know truth. Therefore man's
15 ultimate happiness cannot be in this life.

For these and like reasons Alexander and Averroes held that man's ultimate happiness does not consist in human knowledge obtained through speculative sciences, but in that which results from conjunction with a separate substance, which conjunction
20 they deemed possible to man in this life. But as Aristotle realized that man has no knowledge in this life other than that which he obtains through speculative sciences, he maintained that man attains to happiness, not perfect, but proportionate to his capacity.

Hence it becomes sufficiently clear how these great minds
25 suffered from being so straitened on every side. We, however, will avoid these straits if we suppose, in accordance with the foregoing arguments, that man is able to reach perfect happiness after this life, since man has an immortal soul; and that in that state his soul will understand in the same way as separate substances
30 understand, as we proved in the Second Book.

Therefore man's ultimate happiness will consist in that knowledge of God which he possesses after this life; a knowledge similar to that by which separate substances know him. Hence our Lord promises us a reward . . . in heaven (Matt. v. 12) and (Matt.
35 xxii. 30) states that the saints shall be as the angels: who always see God in heaven (Matt. xviii. 10).

CHAPTER LI

HOW GOD MAY BE SEEN IN HIS ESSENCE

5   SINCE then it is impossible for a natural desire to be void;—
and it would be were it impossible to arrive at understanding the
divine substance; for all minds desire this naturally:—we must
conclude that it is possible for the divine substance to be seen by
means of the intellect; both by separate intellectual substances,
10   and by our souls.

It is sufficiently clear from what has been said, what manner of
vision this is. For we have proved[1] that the divine substance cannot
be seen by the intellect in any created species. Wherefore if God's
essence be seen at all, it must be that the intellect sees it in the
15   divine essence itself: so that in that vision the divine essence is
both the object and the medium of vision.

Since, however, the intellect is unable to understand any
particular substance, unless it be actuated by some species
informing it, that is the image of the thing understood; someone
20   might deem it impossible for a created intellect to see the very
substance of God in the divine essence as an intelligible species,
inasmuch as the divine essence is self-subsistent, and we have
proved in the First Book[2] that God cannot be the form of anything.

In order to understand this truth, we must note that a self-
25   subsisting substance is either a form alone, or is composed of
matter and form. Accordingly, that which is composed of matter
and form cannot be the form of something else: because the form
therein is already confined to that matter, so that it cannot be the
form of another thing. But that which subsists so as nevertheless to
30   be a form alone, can be the form of something else, provided its
being be such that some other thing can participate in it, as we
have proved concerning the human soul in the Second Book.[3] If,
however, its being cannot be participated in by another, it cannot
be the form of anything; because by its very being it is determined
35   in itself, as material things are by their matter. Now we must
consider this as being the case not only with regard to substantial
or natural being, but also as regards intelligible being. For, since
truth is the perfection of the intellect, that intelligible which is
truth itself, will be a pure form in the genus of intelligible things.
40   This applies solely to God: for, since truth is consequent upon
being, that alone is its own truth, which is its own being; and this
belongs to God alone, as we proved in the Second Book.[4]

Consequently other subsistent intelligibles are not pure forms in the genus of intelligible things, but have a form in a subject: for each of them is a true thing, but not the truth, even as it is a being, but not being itself. It is therefore clear that the divine essence can
5 be compared to the created intellect as an intelligible species by which it understands: which cannot be said of the essence of any separate substance. And yet it cannot be the form of another thing as to its natural being: for it would follow that being united to this other, it would constitute one nature; which is impossible, since
10 the divine essence is perfect in itself in its own nature. Whereas the intelligible species in its union with the intellect, does not constitute a nature, but perfects the intellect to the effect of understanding: and this is not inconsistent with the perfection of the divine essence.

15   This immediate vision of God is promised to us in Holy Writ (1 Cor. xiii. 12): We see now through a glass in a dark manner; but then face to face. It would be impious to understand this in a material way, and imagine a material face in the Godhead: since we have proved[5] that God has no body. Nor is it possible for us to
20 see God with a bodily face since the eyes of the body, which are situate in the face, can only see bodily things. Thus then shall we see God face to face, because we shall see Him immediately, even as a man whom we see face to face.

It is according to this vision that we become most like unto
25 God, and participators of His bliss: since God understands His substance by His essence, and this is His bliss. Wherefore it is said (1 Jo. iii. 2): When He shall appear, we shall be like to Him; because we shall see Him as He is. And (Luke xxii. 29, 30) our Lord said: I dispose to you, as My Father hath disposed to Me, a
30 banquet,[6] that you may eat and drink at My table in My kingdom. Now these words cannot be understood as referring to the food and drink of the body, but to that which is taken from the table of Wisdom, of which Wisdom says (Prov. ix. 5): Eat my bread and drink the wine which I have mingled for you. Accordingly, to eat
35 and drink at God's table is to enjoy the same bliss as that which makes God happy, and to see God as He sees Himself.

Notes:

1. Ch. xlix.
2. Ch. xxvi. seqq.
3. Ch. lxviii.
4. Ch. xv.
5. Bk. I., ch. xxvii.
6. Vulg., kingdom.

CHAPTER LXIII

5   ## HOW IN THAT ULTIMATE HAPPINESS
MAN'S EVERY DESIRE IS FULFILLED

IT is evident from what has been said, that in this happy state
which results from the divine vision, man's every desire is
10 fulfilled, according to Ps. cii. 5, Who satisfieth thy desire with
good things, and his every end achieved. This is clear to anyone
who considers man's various desires in kind.

There is a desire in man, as an intellectual being, to know the
truth: and men pursue this desire by the study of the
15 contemplative life. And this will be most clearly fulfilled in that
vision, when the intellect by gazing on the First Truth will know
all that it naturally desires to know, as we have proved above.[1]

There is also a desire in man as a rational being capable of
regulating things beneath him: and he pursues this desire in the
20 occupations of the active and civic life. The chief object of this
desire is that man's entire life be regulated in accord with reason,
to wit, that he may live according to virtue: because the end of
every virtuous man in all his actions is the good of his own virtue,
that of the brave man, for instance, that he may act bravely. Now
25 this desire will then be wholly fulfilled: because the reason will be
right vigorous, being enlightened with the very light of God lest it
stray from righteousness.

Consequent to his life as a citizen, there are also certain goods
that man needs for his civic actions. Such is a position of honour,
30 through inordinate desire of which, men become proud and
ambitious. Now by this vision men are raised to the highest
position of honour, because in a way, they are united to God, as
we have proved above.[2] Hence, even as God Himself is the King of
ages,[3] so the Blessed united to Him are said to be kings (Apoc. xx.
35 6): They shall reign with Christ.

There is another desirable thing consequent to the civic life,
and this is to be well known; through inordinate desire of which
men are said to be desirous of vain glory. Now by this vision the
Blessed become well known, not in the opinion of men, who can
40 both deceive and be deceived, but in the most true knowledge
both of God and of all the Blessed. Hence this happiness is many

times described as glory in Holy Writ: thus it is said in the Psalm (cxlix. 5): The saints shall rejoice in glory.

There is yet another desirable thing in the civic life, and this is riches; through inordinate desire of which men become illiberal
5 and unjust. Now in that happy state there is a sufficiency of all goods: inasmuch as the Blessed enjoy him who contains the perfection of all goods. Hence it is said (Wis. vii. 11): All good things came to me together with her: wherefore it is said again (Ps. cxi. 3): Glory and wealth shall be in his house.
10 There is a third desire in man, common to him and other animals, namely the desire for the enjoyment of pleasure: and this men pursue especially by leading a voluptuous life, and through lack of moderation become intemperate and incontinent. Now in that vision there is the most perfect pleasure, all the more perfect
15 than sensuous pleasure, as the intellect is above the senses; as the good in which we shall delight surpasses all sensible good, is more penetrating, and more continuously delightful; and as that pleasure is freer from all alloy of sorrow, or trouble of anxiety: whereof it is said (Ps. xxxv. 9): They shall be inebriated with the
20 plenty of Thy house, and Thou shalt make them drink of the torrent of Thy pleasure. There is also the natural desire, common to all things, whereby all things seek to be preserved in their being, as far as possible: and through lack of moderation in this desire, men become timorous, and spare themselves overmuch in
25 the matter of labour. This desire will be altogether fulfilled when the Blessed obtain perfect immortality, and security from all evil, according to Is. xlix. 10 and Apoc. xxi. 4:[4] They shall no more hunger or thirst, neither shall the sun fall on them, nor any heat. It is therefore evident that intellectual substances by seeing God
30 attain to true beatitude, when their every desire is satisfied, and when there is a sufficiency of all good things, as is required for happiness, as Aristotle says (10 Ethic. vii. 3). Hence Boethius says (3 De Consol.) that happiness is a state of life made perfect by the accumulation of all goods.
35 In this life there is nothing so like this ultimate and perfect happiness as the life of those who contemplate the truth, as far as possible here below. Hence the philosophers who were unable to obtain full knowledge of that final beatitude, placed man's ultimate happiness in that contemplation which is possible during
40 this life. For this reason too, Holy Writ commends the contemplative rather than other forms of life, when our Lord said (Luke x. 42): Mary hath chosen the better part, namely the

contemplation of truth, which shall not be taken from her. For contemplation of truth begins in this life, but will be consummated in the life to come: while the active and civic life does not transcend the limits of this life.

5

Notes:

1. Ch. lix.
2. Ch. li.
3. 1 Tim. i. 17.
4. Apoc. vii. 16.

SUMMA THEOLOGIAE

FIRST PART

QUESTION 1: The Nature and Extent of Sacred Doctrine

Article 1. Whether, besides philosophy, any further doctrine is required?

Objection 1. It seems that, besides philosophical science, we have no need of any further knowledge. For man should not seek to know what is above reason: "Seek not the things that are too high for thee" (Sirach 3:22). But whatever is not above reason is

5 fully treated of in philosophical science. Therefore any other knowledge besides philosophical science is superfluous.

Objection 2. Further, knowledge can be concerned only with being, for nothing can be known, save what is true; and all that is, is true. But everything that is, is treated of in philosophical

10 science—even God Himself; so that there is a part of philosophy called theology, or the divine science, as Aristotle has proved (Metaph. vi). Therefore, besides philosophical science, there is no need of any further knowledge.

On the contrary, It is written (2 Timothy 3:16): "All

15 Scripture, inspired of God is profitable to teach, to reprove, to correct, to instruct in justice." Now Scripture, inspired of God, is no part of philosophical science, which has been built up by human reason. Therefore it is useful that besides philosophical science, there should be other knowledge, i.e. inspired of God.

20 **I answer that**, It was necessary for man's salvation that there should be a knowledge revealed by God besides philosophical science built up by human reason. Firstly, indeed, because man is directed to God, as to an end that surpasses the grasp of his reason: "The eye hath not seen, O God, besides Thee,

25 what things Thou hast prepared for them that wait for Thee" (Isaiah 64:4). But the end must first be known by men who are to direct their thoughts and actions to the end. Hence it was necessary for the salvation of man that certain truths which exceed

human reason should be made known to him by divine revelation. Even as regards those truths about God which human reason could have discovered, it was necessary that man should be taught by a divine revelation; because the truth about God such as reason
5 could discover, would only be known by a few, and that after a long time, and with the admixture of many errors. Whereas man's whole salvation, which is in God, depends upon the knowledge of this truth. Therefore, in order that the salvation of men might be brought about more fitly and more surely, it was necessary that
10 they should be taught divine truths by divine revelation. It was therefore necessary that besides philosophical science built up by reason, there should be a sacred science learned through revelation.

    Reply to Objection 1. Although those things which are
15 beyond man's knowledge may not be sought for by man through his reason, nevertheless, once they are revealed by God, they must be accepted by faith. Hence the sacred text continues, "For many things are shown to thee above the understanding of man" (Sirach 3:25). And in this, the sacred science consists.

20   **Reply to Objection** 2. Sciences are differentiated according to the various means through which knowledge is obtained. For the astronomer and the physicist both may prove the same conclusion: that the earth, for instance, is round: the astronomer by means of mathematics (i.e. abstracting from matter), but the
25 physicist by means of matter itself. Hence there is no reason why those things which may be learned from philosophical science, so far as they can be known by natural reason, may not also be taught us by another science so far as they fall within revelation. Hence theology included in sacred doctrine differs in kind from that
30 theology which is part of philosophy.

Article 2. Whether sacred doctrine is a science?

35   **Objection** 1. It seems that sacred doctrine is not a science. For every science proceeds from self-evident principles. But sacred doctrine proceeds from articles of faith which are not self-evident, since their truth is not admitted by all: "For all men have not faith" (2 Thessalonians 3:2). Therefore sacred doctrine is not a
40 science.

    Objection 2. Further, no science deals with individual facts. But this sacred science treats of individual facts, such as the deeds of Abraham, Isaac and Jacob and such like. Therefore sacred doctrine is not a science.

On the contrary, Augustine says (De Trin. xiv, 1) "to this science alone belongs that whereby saving faith is begotten,
5   nourished, protected and strengthened." But this can be said of no science except sacred doctrine. Therefore sacred doctrine is a science.

I answer that, Sacred doctrine is a science. We must bear in mind that there are two kinds of sciences. There are some which
10   proceed from a principle known by the natural light of intelligence, such as arithmetic and geometry and the like. There are some which proceed from principles known by the light of a higher science: thus the science of perspective proceeds from principles established by geometry, and music from principles
15   established by arithmetic. So it is that sacred doctrine is a science because it proceeds from principles established by the light of a higher science, namely, the science of God and the blessed. Hence, just as the musician accepts on authority the principles taught him by the mathematician, so sacred science is established
20   on principles revealed by God.

Reply to Objection 1. The principles of any science are either in themselves self-evident, or reducible to the conclusions of a higher science; and such, as we have said, are the principles of sacred doctrine.
25   **Reply to Objection 2**. Individual facts are treated of in sacred doctrine, not because it is concerned with them principally, but they are introduced rather both as examples to be followed in our lives (as in moral sciences) and in order to establish the authority of those men through whom the divine revelation, on
30   which this sacred scripture or doctrine is based, has come down to us.

Article 3. Whether sacred doctrine is one science?

35

Objection 1. It seems that sacred doctrine is not one science; for according to the Philosopher (Poster. i) "that science is one which treats only of one class of subjects." But the creator and the creature, both of whom are treated of in sacred doctrine,
40   cannot be grouped together under one class of subjects. Therefore sacred doctrine is not one science.

Objection 2. Further, in sacred doctrine we treat of angels, corporeal creatures and human morality. But these belong to separate philosophical sciences. Therefore sacred doctrine cannot be one science.

5   **On the contrary**, Holy Scripture speaks of it as one science: "Wisdom gave him the knowledge [scientiam] of holy things" (Wisdom 10:10).

I answer that, Sacred doctrine is one science. The unity of a faculty or habit is to be gauged by its object, not indeed, in its
10   material aspect, but as regards the precise formality under which it is an object. For example, man, ass, stone agree in the one precise formality of being colored; and color is the formal object of sight. Therefore, because Sacred Scripture considers things precisely under the formality of being divinely revealed, whatever has been
15   divinely revealed possesses the one precise formality of the object of this science; and therefore is included under sacred doctrine as under one science.

Reply to Objection 1. Sacred doctrine does not treat of God and creatures equally, but of God primarily, and of creatures
20   only so far as they are referable to God as their beginning or end. Hence the unity of this science is not impaired.

Reply to Objection 2. Nothing prevents inferior faculties or habits from being differentiated by something which falls under a higher faculty or habit as well; because the higher faculty or habit
25   regards the object in its more universal formality, as the object of the "common sense" is whatever affects the senses, including, therefore, whatever is visible or audible. Hence the "common sense", although one faculty, extends to all the objects of the five senses. Similarly, objects which are the subject-matter of different
30   philosophical sciences can yet be treated of by this one single sacred science under one aspect precisely so far as they can be included in revelation. So that in this way, sacred doctrine bears, as it were, the stamp of the divine science which is one and simple, yet extends to everything.

35

Article 4. Whether sacred doctrine is a practical science?

Objection 1. It seems that sacred doctrine is a practical
40   science; for a practical science is that which ends in action according to the Philosopher (Metaph. ii). But sacred doctrine is ordained to action: "Be ye doers of the word, and not hearers

only" (James 1:22). Therefore sacred doctrine is a practical science.

Objection 2. Further, sacred doctrine is divided into the Old and the New Law. But law implies a moral science which is a
5   practical science. Therefore sacred doctrine is a practical science.

On the contrary, Every practical science is concerned with human operations; as moral science is concerned with human acts, and architecture with buildings. But sacred doctrine is chiefly concerned with God, whose handiwork is especially man.
10 Therefore it is not a practical but a speculative science.

I answer that, Sacred doctrine, being one, extends to things which belong to different philosophical sciences because it considers in each the same formal aspect, namely, so far as they can be known through divine revelation. Hence, although among
15 the philosophical sciences one is speculative and another practical, nevertheless sacred doctrine includes both; as God, by one and the same science, knows both Himself and His works. Still, it is speculative rather than practical because it is more concerned with divine things than with human acts; though it does treat even of
20 these latter, inasmuch as man is ordained by them to the perfect knowledge of God in which consists eternal bliss. This is a sufficient answer to the Objections.

25   *Article 5. Whether sacred doctrine is nobler than other*
sciences?

Objection 1. It seems that sacred doctrine is not nobler than other sciences; for the nobility of a science depends on the
30 certitude it establishes. But other sciences, the principles of which cannot be doubted, seem to be more certain than sacred doctrine; for its principles — namely, articles of faith — can be doubted. Therefore other sciences seem to be nobler.

Objection 2. Further, it is the sign of a lower science to
35 depend upon a higher; as music depends on arithmetic. But sacred doctrine does in a sense depend upon philosophical sciences; for Jerome observes, in his Epistle to Magnus, that "the ancient doctors so enriched their books with the ideas and phrases of the philosophers, that thou knowest not what more to admire in
40 them, their profane erudition or their scriptural learning." Therefore sacred doctrine is inferior to other sciences.

On the contrary, Other sciences are called the handmaidens of this one: "Wisdom sent her maids to invite to the tower" (Proverbs 9:3).

I answer that, Since this science is partly speculative and
5 partly practical, it transcends all others speculative and practical. Now one speculative science is said to be nobler than another, either by reason of its greater certitude, or by reason of the higher worth of its subject-matter. In both these respects this science surpasses other speculative sciences; in point of greater certitude,
10 because other sciences derive their certitude from the natural light of human reason, which can err; whereas this derives its certitude from the light of divine knowledge, which cannot be misled: in point of the higher worth of its subject-matter because this science treats chiefly of those things which by their sublimity transcend
15 human reason; while other sciences consider only those things which are within reason's grasp. Of the practical sciences, that one is nobler which is ordained to a further purpose, as political science is nobler than military science; for the good of the army is directed to the good of the State. But the purpose of this science,
20 in so far as it is practical, is eternal bliss; to which as to an ultimate end the purposes of every practical science are directed. Hence it is clear that from every standpoint, it is nobler than other sciences.

Reply to Objection 1. It may well happen that what is in itself the more certain may seem to us the less certain on account
25 of the weakness of our intelligence, "which is dazzled by the clearest objects of nature; as the owl is dazzled by the light of the sun" (Metaph. ii, lect. i). Hence the fact that some happen to doubt about articles of faith is not due to the uncertain nature of the truths, but to the weakness of human intelligence; yet the
30 slenderest knowledge that may be obtained of the highest things is more desirable than the most certain knowledge obtained of lesser things, as is said in de Animalibus xi.

Reply to Objection 2. This science can in a sense depend upon the philosophical sciences, not as though it stood in need of
35 them, but only in order to make its teaching clearer. For it accepts its principles not from other sciences, but immediately from God, by revelation. Therefore it does not depend upon other sciences as upon the higher, but makes use of them as of the lesser, and as handmaidens: even so the master sciences make use of the sciences
40 that supply their materials, as political of military science. That it thus uses them is not due to its own defect or insufficiency, but to the defect of our intelligence, which is more easily led by what is

known through natural reason (from which proceed the other sciences) to that which is above reason, such as are the teachings of this science.

5

Article 6. Whether this doctrine is the same as wisdom?

Objection 1. It seems that this doctrine is not the same as wisdom. For no doctrine which borrows its principles is worthy of 10 the name of wisdom; seeing that the wise man directs, and is not directed (Metaph. i). But this doctrine borrows its principles. Therefore this science is not wisdom.

Objection 2. Further, it is a part of wisdom to prove the principles of other sciences. Hence it is called the chief of sciences, 15 as is clear in Ethic. vi. But this doctrine does not prove the principles of other sciences. Therefore it is not the same as wisdom.

Objection 3. Further, this doctrine is acquired by study, whereas wisdom is acquired by God's inspiration; so that it is 20 numbered among the gifts of the Holy Spirit (Isaiah 11:2). Therefore this doctrine is not the same as wisdom.

On the contrary, It is written (Deuteronomy 4:6): "This is your wisdom and understanding in the sight of nations."

I answer that, This doctrine is wisdom above all human 25 wisdom; not merely in any one order, but absolutely. For since it is the part of a wise man to arrange and to judge, and since lesser matters should be judged in the light of some higher principle, he is said to be wise in any one order who considers the highest principle in that order: thus in the order of building, he who plans 30 the form of the house is called wise and architect, in opposition to the inferior laborers who trim the wood and make ready the stones: "As a wise architect, I have laid the foundation" (1 Corinthians 3:10). Again, in the order of all human life, the prudent man is called wise, inasmuch as he directs his acts to a 35 fitting end: "Wisdom is prudence to a man" (Proverbs 10:23). Therefore he who considers absolutely the highest cause of the whole universe, namely God, is most of all called wise. Hence wisdom is said to be the knowledge of divine things, as Augustine says (De Trin. xii, 14). But sacred doctrine essentially treats of 40 God viewed as the highest cause — not only so far as He can be known through creatures just as philosophers knew Him — "That which is known of God is manifest in them" (Romans 1:19) — but also as far as He is known to Himself alone and revealed to others. Hence sacred doctrine is especially called wisdom.

Reply to Objection 1. Sacred doctrine derives its principles not from any human knowledge, but from the divine knowledge, 5 through which, as through the highest wisdom, all our knowledge is set in order.

Reply to Objection 2. The principles of other sciences either are evident and cannot be proved, or are proved by natural reason through some other science. But the knowledge proper to 10 this science comes through revelation and not through natural reason. Therefore it has no concern to prove the principles of other sciences, but only to judge of them. Whatsoever is found in other sciences contrary to any truth of this science must be condemned as false: "Destroying counsels and every height that 15 exalteth itself against the knowledge of God" (2 Corinthians 10:4-5).

Reply to Objection 3. Since judgment appertains to wisdom, the twofold manner of judging produces a twofold wisdom. A man may judge in one way by inclination, as whoever 20 has the habit of a virtue judges rightly of what concerns that virtue by his very inclination towards it. Hence it is the virtuous man, as we read, who is the measure and rule of human acts. In another way, by knowledge, just as a man learned in moral science might be able to judge rightly about virtuous acts, though he had not the 25 virtue. The first manner of judging divine things belongs to that wisdom which is set down among the gifts of the Holy Ghost: "The spiritual man judgeth all things" (1 Corinthians 2:15). And Dionysius says (Div. Nom. ii): "Hierotheus is taught not by mere learning, but by experience of divine things." The second manner 30 of judging belongs to this doctrine which is acquired by study, though its principles are obtained by revelation.

Article 7. Whether God is the object of this science?

Objection 1. It seems that God is not the object of this 35 science. For in every science, the nature of its object is presupposed. But this science cannot presuppose the essence of God, for Damascene says (De Fide Orth. i, iv): "It is impossible to define the essence of God." Therefore God is not the object of this science.

Objection 2. Further, whatever conclusions are reached in any science must be comprehended under the object of the science. But in Holy Writ we reach conclusions not only concerning God, but concerning many other things, such as
5 creatures and human morality. Therefore God is not the object of this science.

On the contrary, The object of the science is that of which it principally treats. But in this science, the treatment is mainly about God; for it is called theology, as treating of God. Therefore
10 God is the object of this science.

I answer that, God is the object of this science. The relation between a science and its object is the same as that between a habit or faculty and its object. Now properly speaking, the object of a faculty or habit is the thing under the aspect of which all things are
15 referred to that faculty or habit, as man and stone are referred to the faculty of sight in that they are colored. Hence colored things are the proper objects of sight. But in sacred science, all things are treated of under the aspect of God: either because they are God Himself or because they refer to God as their beginning and end.
20 Hence it follows that God is in very truth the object of this science. This is clear also from the principles of this science, namely, the articles of faith, for faith is about God. The object of the principles and of the whole science must be the same, since the whole science is contained virtually in its principles. Some,
25 however, looking to what is treated of in this science, and not to the aspect under which it is treated, have asserted the object of this science to be something other than God — that is, either things and signs; or the works of salvation; or the whole Christ, as the head and members. Of all these things, in truth, we treat in
30 this science, but so far as they have reference to God.

Reply to Objection 1. Although we cannot know in what consists the essence of God, nevertheless in this science we make use of His effects, either of nature or of grace, in place of a definition, in regard to whatever is treated of in this science
35 concerning God; even as in some philosophical sciences we demonstrate something about a cause from its effect, by taking the effect in place of a definition of the cause.

Reply to Objection 2. Whatever other conclusions are reached in this sacred science are comprehended under God, not
40 as parts or species or accidents but as in some way related to Him.

Article 8. Whether sacred doctrine is a matter of argument?

Objection 1. It seems this doctrine is not a matter of
5 argument. For Ambrose says (De Fide 1): "Put arguments aside
where faith is sought." But in this doctrine, faith especially is
sought: "But these things are written that you may believe" (John
20:31). Therefore sacred doctrine is not a matter of argument.

Objection 2. Further, if it is a matter of argument, the
10 argument is either from authority or from reason. If it is from
authority, it seems unbefitting its dignity, for the proof from
authority is the weakest form of proof. But if it is from reason, this
is unbefitting its end, because, according to Gregory (Hom. 26),
"faith has no merit in those things of which human reason brings its
15 own experience." Therefore sacred doctrine is not a matter of
argument.

On the contrary, The Scripture says that a bishop should
"embrace that faithful word which is according to doctrine, that he
may be able to exhort in sound doctrine and to convince the
20 gainsayers" (Titus 1:9).

I answer that, As other sciences do not argue in proof of
their principles, but argue from their principles to demonstrate
other truths in these sciences: so this doctrine does not argue in
proof of its principles, which are the articles of faith, but from
25 them it goes on to prove something else; as the Apostle from the
resurrection of Christ argues in proof of the general resurrection
(1 Corinthians 15). However, it is to be borne in mind, in regard
to the philosophical sciences, that the inferior sciences neither
prove their principles nor dispute with those who deny them, but
30 leave this to a higher science; whereas the highest of them, viz.
metaphysics, can dispute with one who denies its principles, if
only the opponent will make some concession; but if he concede
nothing, it can have no dispute with him, though it can answer his
objections. Hence Sacred Scripture, since it has no science above
35 itself, can dispute with one who denies its principles only if the
opponent admits some at least of the truths obtained through
divine revelation; thus we can argue with heretics from texts in
Holy Writ, and against those who deny one article of faith, we can
argue from another. If our opponent believes nothing of divine
40 revelation, there is no longer any means of proving the articles of
faith by reasoning, but only of answering his objections — if he
has any — against faith. Since faith rests upon infallible truth, and

since the contrary of a truth can never be demonstrated, it is clear that the arguments brought against faith cannot be demonstrations, but are difficulties that can be answered.

Reply to Objection 1. Although arguments from human
5 reason cannot avail to prove what must be received on faith, nevertheless, this doctrine argues from articles of faith to other truths.

Reply to Objection 2. This doctrine is especially based upon arguments from authority, inasmuch as its principles are
10 obtained by revelation: thus we ought to believe on the authority of those to whom the revelation has been made. Nor does this take away from the dignity of this doctrine, for although the argument from authority based on human reason is the weakest, yet the argument from authority based on divine revelation is the
15 strongest. But sacred doctrine makes use even of human reason, not, indeed, to prove faith (for thereby the merit of faith would come to an end), but to make clear other things that are put forward in this doctrine. Since therefore grace does not destroy nature but perfects it, natural reason should minister to faith as the
20 natural bent of the will ministers to charity. Hence the Apostle says: "Bringing into captivity every understanding unto the obedience of Christ" (2 Corinthians 10:5). Hence sacred doctrine makes use also of the authority of philosophers in those questions in which they were able to know the truth by natural reason, as
25 Paul quotes a saying of Aratus: "As some also of your own poets said: For we are also His offspring" (Acts 17:28). Nevertheless, sacred doctrine makes use of these authorities as extrinsic and probable arguments; but properly uses the authority of the canonical Scriptures as an incontrovertible proof, and the
30 authority of the doctors of the Church as one that may properly be used, yet merely as probable. For our faith rests upon the revelation made to the apostles and prophets who wrote the canonical books, and not on the revelations (if any such there are) made to other doctors. Hence Augustine says (Epis. ad Hieron.
35 xix, 1): "Only those books of Scripture which are called canonical have I learned to hold in such honor as to believe their authors have not erred in any way in writing them. But other authors I so read as not to deem everything in their works to be true, merely on account of their having so thought and written, whatever may
40 have been their holiness and learning."

Article 9. Whether Holy Scripture should use metaphors?

Objection 1. It seems that Holy Scripture should not use metaphors. For that which is proper to the lowest science seems not to befit this science, which holds the highest place of all. But
5 to proceed by the aid of various similitudes and figures is proper to poetry, the least of all the sciences. Therefore it is not fitting that this science should make use of such similitudes.

Objection 2. Further, this doctrine seems to be intended to
10 make truth clear. Hence a reward is held out to those who manifest it: "They that explain me shall have life everlasting" (Sirach 24:31). But by such similitudes truth is obscured. Therefore, to put forward divine truths by likening them to corporeal things does not befit this science.

15 **Objection 3**. Further, the higher creatures are, the nearer they approach to the divine likeness. If therefore any creature be taken to represent God, this representation ought chiefly to be taken from the higher creatures, and not from the lower; yet this is often found in Scriptures.

20 **On the contrary**, It is written (Hosea 12:10): "I have multiplied visions, and I have used similitudes by the ministry of the prophets." But to put forward anything by means of similitudes is to use metaphors. Therefore this sacred science may use metaphors.

25 **I answer that**, It is befitting Holy Writ to put forward divine and spiritual truths by means of comparisons with material things. For God provides for everything according to the capacity of its nature. Now it is natural to man to attain to intellectual truths through sensible objects, because all our knowledge
30 originates from sense. Hence in Holy Writ, spiritual truths are fittingly taught under the likeness of material things. This is what Dionysius says (Coel. Hier. i): "We cannot be enlightened by the divine rays except they be hidden within the covering of many sacred veils." It is also befitting Holy Writ, which is proposed to
35 all without distinction of persons — "To the wise and to the unwise I am a debtor" (Romans 1:14) — that spiritual truths be expounded by means of figures taken from corporeal things, in order that thereby even the simple who are unable by themselves to grasp intellectual things may be able to understand it.

40 **Reply to Objection 1**. Poetry makes use of metaphors to produce a representation, for it is natural to man to be pleased

with representations. But sacred doctrine makes use of metaphors as both necessary and useful.

Reply to Objection 2. The ray of divine revelation is not extinguished by the sensible imagery wherewith it is veiled, as
5 Dionysius says (*Coel. Hier.* i); and its truth so far remains that it does not allow the minds of those to whom the revelation has been made, to rest in the metaphors, but raises them to the knowledge of truths; and through those to whom the revelation has been made others also may receive instruction in these matters. Hence
10 those things that are taught metaphorically in one part of Scripture, in other parts are taught more openly. The very hiding of truth in figures is useful for the exercise of thoughtful minds and as a defense against the ridicule of the impious, according to the words "Give not that which is holy to dogs" (Matthew 7:6).
15 **Reply to Objection 3**. As Dionysius says, (*Coel. Hier.* i) it is more fitting that divine truths should be expounded under the figure of less noble than of nobler bodies, and this for three reasons. Firstly, because thereby men's minds are the better preserved from error. For then it is clear that these things are not
20 literal descriptions of divine truths, which might have been open to doubt had they been expressed under the figure of nobler bodies, especially for those who could think of nothing nobler than bodies. Secondly, because this is more befitting the knowledge of God that we have in this life. For what He is not is clearer to us
25 than what He is. Therefore similitudes drawn from things farthest away from God form within us a truer estimate that God is above whatsoever we may say or think of Him. Thirdly, because thereby divine truths are the better hidden from the unworthy.

30

Article 10. Whether in Holy Scripture a word may have several senses?

Objection 1. It seems that in Holy Writ a word cannot have
35 several senses, historical or literal, allegorical, tropological or moral, and anagogical. For many different senses in one text produce confusion and deception and destroy all force of argument. Hence no argument, but only fallacies, can be deduced from a multiplicity of propositions. But Holy Writ ought to be
40 able to state the truth without any fallacy. Therefore in it there cannot be several senses to a word.

Objection 2. Further, Augustine says (*De util. cred.* iii) that "the Old Testament has a fourfold division as to history, etiology, analogy and allegory." Now these four seem altogether different from the four divisions mentioned in the first objection. Therefore
5 it does not seem fitting to explain the same word of Holy Writ according to the four different senses mentioned above.

Objection 3. Further, besides these senses, there is the parabolical, which is not one of these four.

On the contrary, Gregory says (*Moral.* xx, 1): "Holy Writ
10 by the manner of its speech transcends every science, because in one and the same sentence, while it describes a fact, it reveals a mystery."

I answer that, The author of Holy Writ is God, in whose power it is to signify His meaning, not by words only (as man also
15 can do), but also by things themselves. So, whereas in every other science things are signified by words, this science has the property, that the things signified by the words have themselves also a signification. Therefore that first signification whereby words signify things belongs to the first sense, the historical or literal.
20 That signification whereby things signified by words have themselves also a signification is called the spiritual sense, which is based on the literal, and presupposes it. Now this spiritual sense has a threefold division. For as the Apostle says (Hebrews 10:1) the Old Law is a figure of the New Law, and Dionysius says (*Coel.*
25 *Hier.* i) "the New Law itself is a figure of future glory." Again, in the New Law, whatever our Head has done is a type of what we ought to do. Therefore, so far as the things of the Old Law signify the things of the New Law, there is the allegorical sense; so far as the things done in Christ, or so far as the things which signify
30 Christ, are types of what we ought to do, there is the moral sense. But so far as they signify what relates to eternal glory, there is the anagogical sense. Since the literal sense is that which the author intends, and since the author of Holy Writ is God, Who by one act comprehends all things by His intellect, it is not unfitting, as
35 Augustine says (*Confess.* xii), if, even according to the literal sense, one word in Holy Writ should have several senses.

Reply to Objection 1. The multiplicity of these senses does not produce equivocation or any other kind of multiplicity, seeing that these senses are not multiplied because one word signifies
40 several things, but because the things signified by the words can be themselves types of other things. Thus in Holy Writ no confusion results, for all the senses are founded on one — the literal —

from which alone can any argument be drawn, and not from those intended in allegory, as Augustine says (Epis. 48). Nevertheless, nothing of Holy Scripture perishes on account of this, since nothing necessary to faith is contained under the spiritual sense
5   which is not elsewhere put forward by the Scripture in its literal sense.

Reply to Objection 2. These three — history, etiology, analogy — are grouped under the literal sense. For it is called history, as Augustine expounds (Epis. 48), whenever anything is
10   simply related; it is called etiology when its cause is assigned, as when Our Lord gave the reason why Moses allowed the putting away of wives — namely, on account of the hardness of men's hearts; it is called analogy whenever the truth of one text of Scripture is shown not to contradict the truth of another. Of these
15   four, allegory alone stands for the three spiritual senses. Thus Hugh of St. Victor (*Sacram*. iv, 4 Prolog.) includes the anagogical under the allegorical sense, laying down three senses only — the historical, the allegorical, and the tropological.

Reply to Objection 3. The parabolical sense is contained in
20   the literal, for by words things are signified properly and figuratively. Nor is the figure itself, but that which is figured, the literal sense. When Scripture speaks of God's arm, the literal sense is not that God has such a member, but only what is signified by this member, namely operative power. Hence it is plain that
25   nothing false can ever underlie the literal sense of Holy Writ.

QUESTION 2: On God's Existence

Article 1: *Whether the existence of God is self-evident?*

Objection 1. It seems that the existence of God is self-evident. Now those things are said to be self-evident to us the
30   knowledge of which is naturally implanted in us, as we can see in

regard to first principles. But as Damascene says (*De Fide Orth*. i, 1,3), "the knowledge of God is naturally implanted in all." Therefore the existence of God is self-evident.

Objection 2. Further, those things are said to be self-evident
5 which are known as soon as the terms are known, which the Philosopher (*1 Poster*. iii) says is true of the first principles of demonstration. Thus, when the nature of a whole and of a part is known, it is at once recognized that every whole is greater than its part. But as soon as the signification of the word "God" is
10 understood, it is at once seen that God exists. For by this word is signified that thing than which nothing greater can be conceived. But that which exists actually and mentally is greater than that which exists only mentally. Therefore, since as soon as the word "God" is understood it exists mentally, it also follows that it exists
15 actually. Therefore the proposition "God exists" is self-evident.

Objection 3. Further, the existence of truth is self-evident. For whoever denies the existence of truth grants that truth does not exist: and, if truth does not exist, then the proposition "Truth does not exist" is true: and if there is anything true, there must be
20 truth. But God is truth itself: "I am the way, the truth, and the life" (Jn. 14:6) Therefore "God exists" is self-evident.

On the contrary, No one can mentally admit the opposite of what is self-evident; as the Philosopher (*Metaph*. iv, lect. vi) states concerning the first principles of demonstration. But the
25 opposite of the proposition "God is" can be mentally admitted: "The fool said in his heart, There is no God" (Ps. 52:1). Therefore, that God exists is not self-evident.

I answer that, A thing can be self-evident in either of two ways: on the one hand, self-evident in itself, though not to us; on
30 the other, self-evident in itself, and to us. A proposition is self-evident because the predicate is included in the essence of the subject, as "Man is an animal," for animal is contained in the essence of man. If, therefore the essence of the predicate and subject be known to all, the proposition will be self-evident to all;
35 as is clear with regard to the first principles of demonstration, the terms of which are common things that no one is ignorant of, such as being and non-being, whole and part, and such like. If, however, there are some to whom the essence of the predicate and subject is unknown, the proposition will be self-evident in
40 itself, but not to those who do not know the meaning of the predicate and subject of the proposition. Therefore, it happens, as Boethius says (*Hebdom*., the title of which is: "Whether all that is,

is good"), "that there are some mental concepts self-evident only to the learned, as that incorporeal substances are not in space." Therefore I say that this proposition, "God exists," of itself is self-evident, for the predicate is the same as the subject, because God
5 is His own existence as will be hereafter shown (3, 4). Now because we do not know the essence of God, the proposition is not self-evident to us; but needs to be demonstrated by things that are more known to us, though less known in their nature—namely, by effects.

10   **Reply to Objection 1.** To know that God exists in a general and confused way is implanted in us by nature, inasmuch as God is man's beatitude. For man naturally desires happiness, and what is naturally desired by man must be naturally known to him. This, however, is not to know absolutely that God exists; just as to
15 know that someone is approaching is not the same as to know that Peter is approaching, even though it is Peter who is approaching; for many there are who imagine that man's perfect good which is happiness, consists in riches, and others in pleasures, and others in something else.

20   **Reply to Objection 2.** Perhaps not everyone who hears this word "God" understands it to signify something than which nothing greater can be thought, seeing that some have believed God to be a body. Yet, granted that everyone understands that by this word "God" is signified something than which nothing greater
25 can be thought, nevertheless, it does not therefore follow that he understands that what the word signifies exists actually, but only that it exists mentally. Nor can it be argued that it actually exists, unless it be admitted that there actually exists something than which nothing greater can be thought; and this precisely is not
30 admitted by those who hold that God does not exist.

    Reply to Objection 3. The existence of truth in general is self-evident but the existence of a Primal Truth is not self-evident to us.

35

Article 2: *Whether it can be demonstrated that God exists?*

    Objection 1. It seems that the existence of God cannot be demonstrated. For it is an article of faith that God exists. But what
40 is of faith cannot be demonstrated, because a demonstration produces scientific knowledge; whereas faith is of the unseen (Heb. 11:1). Therefore it cannot be demonstrated that God exists.

Objection 2. Further, the essence is the middle term of demonstration. But we cannot know in what God's essence consists, but solely in what it does not consist; as Damascene says (*De Fide Orth*. i, 4). Therefore we cannot demonstrate that God
5 exists.

Objection 3. Further, if the existence of God were demonstrated, this could only be from His effects. But His effects are not proportionate to Him, since He is infinite and His effects are finite; and between the finite and infinite there is no
10 proportion. Therefore, since a cause cannot be demonstrated by an effect not proportionate to it, it seems that the existence of God cannot be demonstrated.

On the contrary, The Apostle says: "The invisible things of Him are clearly seen, being understood by the things that are
15 made" (Rm. 1:20). But this would not be unless the existence of God could be demonstrated through the things that are made; for the first thing we must know of anything is whether it exists.

I answer that, Demonstration can be made in two ways: One is through the cause, and is called "*a priori*," and this is to
20 argue from what is prior absolutely. The other is through the effect, and is called a demonstration "*a posteriori*"; this is to argue from what is prior relatively only to us. When an effect is better known to us than its cause, from the effect we proceed to the knowledge of the cause. And from every effect the existence of its
25 proper cause can be demonstrated, so long as its effects are better known to us; because since every effect depends upon its cause, if the effect exists, the cause must pre-exist. Hence the existence of God, in so far as it is not self-evident to us, can be demonstrated from those of His effects which are known to us.

30 **Reply to Objection 1.** The existence of God and other like truths about God, which can be known by natural reason, are not articles of faith, but are preambles to the articles; for faith presupposes natural knowledge, even as grace presupposes nature, and perfection supposes something that can be perfected.
35 Nevertheless, there is nothing to prevent a man, who cannot grasp a proof, accepting, as a matter of faith, something which in itself is capable of being scientifically known and demonstrated.

Reply to Objection 2. When the existence of a cause is demonstrated from an effect, this effect takes the place of the
40 definition of the cause in proof of the cause's existence. This is especially the case in regard to God, because, in order to prove the existence of anything, it is necessary to accept as a middle term

the meaning of the word, and not its essence, for the question of its essence follows on the question of its existence. Now the names given to God are derived from His effects; consequently, in demonstrating the existence of God from His effects, we may take
5 for the middle term the meaning of the word "God".

Reply to Objection 3. From effects not proportionate to the cause no perfect knowledge of that cause can be obtained. Yet from every effect the existence of the cause can be clearly demonstrated, and so we can demonstrate the existence of God
10 from His effects; though from them we cannot perfectly know God as He is in His essence.

ARTICLE 3: *Whether God exists?*
15

Objection 1. It seems that God does not exist; because if one of two contraries be infinite, the other would be altogether destroyed. But the word "God" means that He is infinite goodness. If, therefore, God existed, there would be no evil discoverable;
20 but there is evil in the world. Therefore God does not exist.

Objection 2. Further, it is superfluous to suppose that what can be accounted for by a few principles has been produced by many. But it seems that everything we see in the world can be accounted for by other principles, supposing God did not exist.
25 For all natural things can be reduced to one principle which is nature; and all voluntary things can be reduced to one principle which is human reason, or will. Therefore there is no need to suppose God's existence.

On the contrary, It is said in the person of God: "I am Who
30 am." (Exodus 3:14)

I answer that, The existence of God can be proved in five ways.

The first and more manifest way is the argument from motion. It is certain, and evident to our senses, that in the world
35 some things are in motion. Now whatever is in motion is put in motion by another, for nothing can be in motion except it is in potentiality to that towards which it is in motion; whereas a thing moves inasmuch as it is in act. For motion is nothing else than the reduction of something from potentiality to actuality. But nothing
40 can be reduced from potentiality to actuality, except by something in a state of actuality. Thus that which is actually hot, as fire, makes wood, which is potentially hot, to be actually hot, and

thereby moves and changes it. Now it is not possible that the same thing should be at once in actuality and potentiality in the same respect, but only in different respects. For what is actually hot cannot simultaneously be potentially hot; but it is simultaneously

5 potentially cold. It is therefore impossible that in the same respect and in the same way a thing should be both mover and moved, i.e. that it should move itself. Therefore, whatever is in motion must be put in motion by another. If that by which it is put in motion be itself put in motion, then this also must needs be put in motion by

10 another, and that by another again. But this cannot go on to infinity, because then there would be no first mover, and, consequently, no other mover; seeing that subsequent movers move only inasmuch as they are put in motion by the first mover; as the staff moves only because it is put in motion by the hand.

15 Therefore it is necessary to arrive at a first mover, put in motion by no other; and this everyone understands to be God.

The second way is from the nature of the efficient cause. In the world of sense we find there is an order of efficient causes. There is no case known (neither is it, indeed, possible) in which a

20 thing is found to be the efficient cause of itself; for so it would be prior to itself, which is impossible. Now in efficient causes it is not possible to go on to infinity, because in all efficient causes following in order, the first is the cause of the intermediate cause, and the intermediate is the cause of the ultimate cause, whether

25 the intermediate cause be several, or only one. Now to take away the cause is to take away the effect. Therefore, if there be no first cause among efficient causes, there will be no ultimate, nor any intermediate cause. But if in efficient causes it is possible to go on to infinity, there will be no first efficient cause, neither will there

30 be an ultimate effect, nor any intermediate efficient causes; all of which is plainly false. Therefore it is necessary to admit a first efficient cause, to which everyone gives the name of God.

The third way is taken from possibility and necessity, and runs thus. We find in nature things that are possible to be and not to

35 be, since they are found to be generated, and to corrupt, and consequently, they are possible to be and not to be. But it is impossible for these always to exist, for that which is possible not to be at some time is not. Therefore, if everything is possible not to be, then at one time there could have been nothing in

40 existence. Now if this were true, even now there would be nothing in existence, because that which does not exist only begins to exist by something already existing. Therefore, if at one time

nothing was in existence, it would have been impossible for anything to have begun to exist; and thus even now nothing would be in existence—which is absurd. Therefore, not all beings are merely possible, but there must exist something the existence of 5 which is necessary. But every necessary thing either has its necessity caused by another, or not. Now it is impossible to go on to infinity in necessary things which have their necessity caused by another, as has been already proved in regard to efficient causes. Therefore we cannot but postulate the existence of some being 10 having of itself its own necessity, and not receiving it from another, but rather causing in others their necessity. This all men speak of as God.

The fourth way is taken from the gradation to be found in things. Among beings there are some more and some less good, 15 true, noble and the like. But "more" and "less" are predicated of different things, according as they resemble in their different ways something which is the maximum, as a thing is said to be hotter according as it more nearly resembles that which is hottest; so that there is something which is truest, something best, something 20 noblest and, consequently, something which is uttermost being; for those things that are greatest in truth are greatest in being, as it is written in *Metaph*. ii. Now the maximum in any genus is the cause of all in that genus; as fire, which is the maximum heat, is the cause of all hot things. Therefore there must also be something 25 which is to all beings the cause of their being, goodness, and every other perfection; and this we call God.

The fifth way is taken from the governance of the world. We see that things which lack intelligence, such as natural bodies, act for an end, and this is evident from their acting always, or nearly 30 always, in the same way, so as to obtain the best result. Hence it is plain that not fortuitously, but designedly, do they achieve their end. Now whatever lacks intelligence cannot move towards an end, unless it be directed by some being endowed with knowledge and intelligence; as the arrow is shot to its mark by the archer. 35 Therefore some intelligent being exists by whom all natural things are directed to their end; and this being we call God.

Reply to Objection 1. As Augustine says (*Enchiridion* xi): "Since God is the highest good, He would not allow any evil to exist in His works, unless His omnipotence and goodness were 40 such as to bring good even out of evil." This is part of the infinite goodness of God, that He should allow evil to exist, and out of it produce good.

Reply to Objection 2. Since nature works for a determinate end under the direction of a higher agent, whatever is done by nature must needs be traced back to God, as to its first cause. So also whatever is done voluntarily must also be traced
5 back to some higher cause other than human reason or will, since these can change or fail; for all things that are changeable and capable of defect must be traced back to an immovable and self-necessary first principle, as was shown in the body of the Article.

10

SECOND PART OF THE SECOND PART

5 ### Question 2: The Act of Faith

Article 1. Whether to believe is to think with assent?

Objection 1. It would seem that to believe is not to think
10 with assent. Because the Latin word "cogitatio" [thought] implies a
research, for "cogitare" [to think] seems to be equivalent to
"coagitare," i.e. "to discuss together." Now Damascene says (*De
Fide Orth*. iv) that faith is "an assent without research." Therefore
thinking has no place in the act of faith.
15   **Objection 2**. Further, faith resides in the reason, as we shall
show further on (4, 2). Now to think is an act of the cogitative
power, which belongs to the sensitive faculty, as stated in I, 78, 4.
Therefore thought has nothing to do with faith.
    Objection 3. Further, to believe is an act of the intellect,
20 since its object is truth. But assent seems to be an act not of the
intellect, but of the will, even as consent is, as stated above (I-II,
15, 1, ad 3). Therefore to believe is not to think with assent.
    On the contrary, This is how "to believe" is defined by
Augustine (*De Praedest. Sanct*. ii).
25   **I answer that**, "To think" can be taken in three ways. First, in
a general way for any kind of actual consideration of the intellect,
as Augustine observes (*De Trin*. xiv, 7): "By understanding I mean
now the faculty whereby we understand when thinking."
Secondly, "to think" is more strictly taken for that consideration of
30 the intellect, which is accompanied by some kind of inquiry, and
which precedes the intellect's arrival at the stage of perfection that
comes with the certitude of sight. On this sense Augustine says (*De
Trin*. xv, 16) that "the Son of God is not called the Thought, but
the Word of God. When our thought realizes what we know and
35 takes form therefrom, it becomes our word. Hence the Word of
God must be understood without any thinking on the part of God,
for there is nothing there that can take form, or be unformed." In
this way thought is, properly speaking, the movement of the mind
while yet deliberating, and not yet perfected by the clear sight of
40 truth. Since, however, such a movement of the mind may be one
of deliberation either about universal notions, which belongs to
the intellectual faculty, or about particular matters, which belongs

to the sensitive part, hence it is that "to think" is taken secondly for an act of the deliberating intellect, and thirdly for an act of the cogitative power.

Accordingly, if "to think" be understood broadly according to
5 the first sense, then "to think with assent," does not express completely what is meant by "to believe": since, in this way, a man thinks with assent even when he considers what he knows by science [Science is certain knowledge of a demonstrated conclusion through its demonstration.], or understands. If, on the
10 other hand, "to think" be understood in the second way, then this expresses completely the nature of the act of believing. For among the acts belonging to the intellect, some have a firm assent without any such kind of thinking, as when a man considers the things that he knows by science, or understands, for this consideration is
15 already formed. But some acts of the intellect have unformed thought devoid of a firm assent, whether they incline to neither side, as in one who "doubts"; or incline to one side rather than the other, but on account of some slight motive, as in one who "suspects"; or incline to one side yet with fear of the other, as in
20 one who "opines." But this act "to believe," cleaves firmly to one side, in which respect belief has something in common with science and understanding; yet its knowledge does not attain the perfection of clear sight, wherein it agrees with doubt, suspicion and opinion. Hence it is proper to the believer to think with
25 assent: so that the act of believing is distinguished from all the other acts of the intellect, which are about the true or the false.

Reply to Objection 1. Faith has not that research of natural reason which demonstrates what is believed, but a research into
30 those things whereby a man is induced to believe, for instance that such things have been uttered by God and confirmed by miracles.

Reply to Objection 2. "To think" is not taken here for the act of the cogitative power, but for an act of the intellect, as explained above.

35 **Reply to Objection 3**. The intellect of the believer is determined to one object, not by the reason, but by the will, wherefore assent is taken here for an act of the intellect as determined to one object by the will.

40

Article 2. Whether the act of faith is suitably distinguished as believing God, believing in a God and believing in God?

5   **Objection 1.** It would seem that the act of faith is unsuitably distinguished as believing God, believing in a God, and believing in God. For one habit has but one act. Now faith is one habit since it is one virtue. Therefore it is unreasonable to say that there are three acts of faith.

10   **Objection 2.** Further, that which is common to all acts of faith should not be reckoned as a particular kind of act of faith. Now "to believe God" is common to all acts of faith, since faith is founded on the First Truth. Therefore it seems unreasonable to distinguish it from certain other acts of faith.

15   **Objection 3.** Further, that which can be said of unbelievers, cannot be called an act of faith. Now unbelievers can be said to believe in a God. Therefore it should not be reckoned an act of faith.

    Objection 4. Further, movement towards the end belongs to
20   the will, whose object is the good and the end. Now to believe is an act, not of the will, but of the intellect. Therefore "to believe in God," which implies movement towards an end, should not be reckoned as a species of that act.

    On the contrary is the authority of Augustine who makes
25   this distinction (*De Verb. Dom.*, Serm. lxi—Tract. xxix in Joan.).

    I answer that, The act of any power or habit depends on the relation of that power or habit to its object. Now the object of faith can be considered in three ways. For, since "to believe" is an act of the intellect, in so far as the will moves it to assent, as stated
30   above (1, ad 3), the object of faith can be considered either on the part of the intellect, or on the part of the will that moves the intellect.

    If it be considered on the part of the intellect, then two things can be observed in the object of faith, as stated above (Question 1,
35   Article 1). One of these is the material object of faith, and in this way an act of faith is "to believe in a God"; because, as stated above (Question 1, Article 1) nothing is proposed to our belief, except in as much as it is referred to God. The other is the formal aspect of the object, for it is the medium on account of which we
40   assent to such and such a point of faith; and thus an act of faith is "to believe God," since, as stated above (Question 1, Article 1) the

formal object of faith is the First Truth, to Which man gives his adhesion, so as to assent to Its sake to whatever he believes.

Thirdly, if the object of faith be considered in so far as the intellect is moved by the will, an act of faith is "to believe in God."
5 For the First Truth is referred to the will, through having the aspect of an end.

Reply to Objection 1. These three do not denote different acts of faith, but one and the same act having different relations to the object of faith.

10   This suffices for the Reply to the Second Objection.

Reply to Objection 3. Unbelievers cannot be said "to believe in a God" as we understand it in relation to the act of faith. For they do not believe that God exists under the conditions that faith determines; hence they do not truly imply believe in a God,
15 since, as the Philosopher observes (*Metaph.* ix, text. 22) "to know simple things defectively is not to know them at all."

Reply to Objection 4. As stated above (I-II, 9, 1) the will moves the intellect and the other powers of the soul to the end: and in this respect an act of faith is "to believe in God."
20

Article 3. Whether it is necessary for salvation to believe anything above the natural reason?

25   **Objection 1.** It would seem unnecessary for salvation to believe anything above the natural reason. For the salvation and perfection of a thing seem to be sufficiently insured by its natural endowments. Now matters of faith, surpass man's natural reason, since they are things unseen as stated above (Question 1, Article
30 4). Therefore to believe seems unnecessary for salvation.

Objection 2. Further, it is dangerous for man to assent to matters, wherein he cannot judge whether that which is proposed to him be true or false, according to Job 12:11: "Doth not the ear discern words?" Now a man cannot form a judgment of this kind
35 in matters of faith, since he cannot trace them back to first principles, by which all our judgments are guided. Therefore it is dangerous to believe in such matters. Therefore to believe is not necessary for salvation.

Objection 3. Further, man's salvation rests on God,
40 according to Psalm 36:39: "But the salvation of the just is from the Lord." Now "the invisible things" of God "are clearly seen, being understood by the things that are made; His eternal power also

and Divinity," according to Romans 1:20: and those things which are clearly seen by the understanding are not an object of belief. Therefore it is not necessary for man's salvation, that he should believe certain things.

5   **On the contrary**, It is written (Hebrews 11:6): "Without faith it is impossible to please God."

       I answer that, Wherever one nature is subordinate to another, we find that two things concur towards the perfection of the lower nature, one of which is in respect of that nature's proper

10   movement, while the other is in respect of the movement of the higher nature. Thus water by its proper movement moves towards the centre (of the earth), while according to the movement of the moon, it moves round the centre by ebb and flow. On like manner the planets have their proper movements from west to

15   east, while in accordance with the movement of the first heaven, they have a movement from east to west. Now the created rational nature alone is immediately subordinate to God, since other creatures do not attain to the universal, but only to something particular, while they partake of the Divine goodness

20   either in "being" only, as inanimate things, or also in "living," and in "knowing singulars," as plants and animals; whereas the rational nature, in as much as it apprehends the universal notion of good and being, is immediately related to the universal principle of being.

25   Consequently the perfection of the rational creature consists not only in what belongs to it in respect of its nature, but also in that which it acquires through a supernatural participation of Divine goodness. Hence it was said above (I-II, 3, 8) that man's ultimate happiness consists in a supernatural vision of God: to

30   which vision man cannot attain unless he be taught by God, according to John 6:45: "Every one that hath heard of the Father and hath learned cometh to Me." Now man acquires a share of this learning, not indeed all at once, but by little and little, according to the mode of his nature: and every one who learns thus must

35   needs believe, in order that he may acquire science in a perfect degree; thus also the Philosopher remarks (*De Soph. Elench.* i, 2) that "it behooves a learner to believe."

       Hence in order that a man arrive at the perfect vision of heavenly happiness, he must first of all believe God, as a disciple

40   believes the master who is teaching him.

       Reply to Objection 1. Since man's nature is dependent on a higher nature, natural knowledge does not suffice for its perfection, and some supernatural knowledge is necessary, as stated above.

Reply to Objection 2. Just as man assents to first principles, by the natural light of his intellect, so does a virtuous man, by the
5 habit of virtue, judge aright of things concerning that virtue; and in this way, by the light of faith which God bestows on him, a man assents to matters of faith and not to those which are against faith. Consequently "there is no" danger or "condemnation to them that are in Christ Jesus," and whom He has enlightened by faith.
10   **Reply to Objection 3.** In many respects faith perceives the invisible things of God in a higher way than natural reason does in proceeding to God from His creatures. Hence it is written (Sirach 3:25): "Many things are shown to thee above the understandings of man."
15

Article 4. Whether it is necessary to believe those things which can be proved by natural reason?

20   **Objection 1.** It would seem unnecessary to believe those things which can be proved by natural reason. For nothing is superfluous in God's works, much less even than in the works of nature. Now it is superfluous to employ other means, where one already suffices. Therefore it would be superfluous to receive by
25 faith, things that can be known by natural reason.

    Objection 2. Further, those things must be believed, which are the object of faith. Now science and faith are not about the same object, as stated above (1, 4,5). Since therefore all things that can be known by natural reason are an object of science, it
30 seems that there is no need to believe what can be proved by natural reason.

    Objection 3. Further, all things knowable scientifically [Science is certain knowledge of a demonstrated conclusion through its demonstration] would seem to come under one head:
35 so that if some of them are proposed to man as objects of faith, in like manner the others should also be believed. But this is not true. Therefore it is not necessary to believe those things which can be proved by natural reason.

    On the contrary, It is necessary to believe that God is one
40 and incorporeal: which things philosophers prove by natural reason.

I answer that, It is necessary for man to accept by faith not only things which are above reason, but also those which can be known by reason: and this for three motives. First, in order that man may arrive more quickly at the knowledge of Divine truth.
5   Because the science to whose province it belongs to prove the existence of God, is the last of all to offer itself to human research, since it presupposes many other sciences: so that it would not by until late in life that man would arrive at the knowledge of God. The second reason is, in order that the knowledge of God may be
10 more general. For many are unable to make progress in the study of science, either through dullness of mind, or through having a number of occupations, and temporal needs, or even through laziness in learning, all of whom would be altogether deprived of the knowledge of God, unless Divine things were brought to their
15 knowledge under the guise of faith. The third reason is for the sake of certitude. For human reason is very deficient in things concerning God. A sign of this is that philosophers in their researches, by natural investigation, into human affairs, have fallen into many errors, and have disagreed among themselves. And
20 consequently, in order that men might have knowledge of God, free of doubt and uncertainty, it was necessary for Divine matters to be delivered to them by way of faith, being told to them, as it were, by God Himself Who cannot lie.

Reply to Objection 1. The researches of natural reason do
25 not suffice mankind for the knowledge of Divine matters, even of those that can be proved by reason: and so it is not superfluous if these others be believed.

Reply to Objection 2. Science and faith cannot be in the same subject and about the same object: but what is an object of
30 science for one, can be an object of faith for another, as stated above (Question 1, Article 5).

Reply to Objection 3. Although all things that can be known by science are of one common scientific aspect, they do not all alike lead man to beatitude: hence they are not all equally
35 proposed to our belief.

Article 5. Whether man is bound to believe anything explicitly?

40

Objection 1. It would seem that man is not bound to believe anything explicitly. For no man is bound to do what is not in his

power. Now it is not in man's power to believe a thing explicitly, for it is written (Romans 10:14-15): "How shall they believe Him, of whom they have not heard? And how shall they hear without a preacher? And how shall they preach unless they be sent?"
5　Therefore man is not bound to believe anything explicitly.

Objection 2. Further, just as we are directed to God by faith, so are we by charity. Now man is not bound to keep the precepts of charity, and it is enough if he be ready to fulfil them: as is evidenced by the precept of Our Lord (Matthew 5:39): "If one
10　strike thee on one [Vulgate: 'thy right'] cheek, turn to him also the other"; and by others of the same kind, according to Augustine's exposition (De Serm. Dom. in Monte xix). Therefore neither is man bound to believe anything explicitly, and it is enough if he be ready to believe whatever God proposes to be believed.

15　**Objection 3.** Further, the good of faith consists in obedience, according to Romans 1:5: "For obedience to the faith in all nations." Now the virtue of obedience does not require man to keep certain fixed precepts, but it is enough that his mind be ready to obey, according to Psalm 118:60: "I am ready and am not
20　troubled; that I may keep Thy commandments." Therefore it seems enough for faith, too, that man should be ready to believe whatever God may propose, without his believing anything explicitly.

On the contrary, It is written (Hebrews 11:6): "He that cometh to God, must believe that He is, and is a rewarder to them
25　that seek Him."

I answer that, The precepts of the Law, which man is bound to fulfill, concern acts of virtue which are the means of attaining salvation. Now an act of virtue, as stated above (I-II, 60, 5)
30　depends on the relation of the habit to its object. Again two things may be considered in the object of any virtue; namely, that which is the proper and direct object of that virtue, and that which is accidental and consequent to the object properly so called. Thus it belongs properly and directly to the object of fortitude, to face the
35　dangers of death, and to charge at the foe with danger to oneself, for the sake of the common good: yet that, in a just war, a man be armed, or strike another with his sword, and so forth, is reduced to the object of fortitude, but indirectly.

Accordingly, just as a virtuous act is required for the fulfillment
40　of a precept, so is it necessary that the virtuous act should terminate in its proper and direct object: but, on the other hand, the fulfilment of the precept does not require that a virtuous act

should terminate in those things which have an accidental or secondary relation to the proper and direct object of that virtue, except in certain places and at certain times. We must, therefore, say that the direct object of faith is that whereby man is made one
5 of the Blessed, as stated above (Question 1, Article 8): while the indirect and secondary object comprises all things delivered by God to us in Holy Writ, for instance that Abraham had two sons, that David was the son of Jesse, and so forth.

Therefore, as regards the primary points or articles of faith,
10 man is bound to believe them, just as he is bound to have faith; but as to other points of faith, man is not bound to believe them explicitly, but only implicitly, or to be ready to believe them, in so far as he is prepared to believe whatever is contained in the Divine Scriptures. Then alone is he bound to believe such things
15 explicitly, when it is clear to him that they are contained in the doctrine of faith.

Reply to Objection 1. If we understand those things alone to be in a man's power, which we can do without the help of grace,
20 then we are bound to do many things which we cannot do without the aid of healing grace, such as to love God and our neighbor, and likewise to believe the articles of faith. But with the help of grace we can do this, for this help "to whomsoever it is given from above it is mercifully given; and from whom it is withheld it is
25 justly withheld, as a punishment of a previous, or at least of original, sin," as Augustine states (*De Corr. et Grat.* v, vi [Cf. Ep. cxc; *De Praed. Sanct.* viii.]).

Reply to Objection 2. Man is bound to love definitely those lovable things which are properly and directly the objects of
30 charity, namely, God and our neighbor. The objection refers to those precepts of charity which belong, as a consequence, to the objects of charity.

Reply to Objection 3. The virtue of obedience is seated, properly speaking, in the will; hence promptness of the will
35 subject to authority, suffices for the act of obedience, because it is the proper and direct object of obedience. But this or that precept is accidental or consequent to that proper and direct object.

Article 6. Whether all are equally bound to have explicit faith?

Objection 1. It would seem that all are equally bound to have
5 explicit faith. For all are bound to those things which are necessary
for salvation, as is evidenced by the precepts of charity. Now it is
necessary for salvation that certain things should be believed
explicitly. Therefore all are equally bound to have explicit faith.

Objection 2. Further, no one should be put to test in matters
10 that he is not bound to believe. But simple reasons are sometimes
tested in reference to the slightest articles of faith. Therefore all
are bound to believe everything explicitly.

Objection 3. Further, if the simple are bound to have, not
explicit but only implicit faith, their faith must needs be implied in
15 the faith of the learned. But this seems unsafe, since it is possible
for the learned to err. Therefore it seems that the simple should
also have explicit faith; so that all are, therefore, equally bound to
have explicit faith.

20   **On the contrary**, It is written (Job 1:14): "The oxen were
ploughing, and the asses feeding beside them," because, as
Gregory expounds this passage (*Moral*. ii, 17), the simple, who are
signified by the asses, ought, in matters of faith, to stay by the
learned, who are denoted by the oxen.

25   **I answer that**, The unfolding of matters of faith is the result
of Divine revelation: for matters of faith surpass natural reason.
Now Divine revelation reaches those of lower degree through
those who are over them, in a certain order; to men, for instance,
through the angels, and to the lower angels through the higher, as
30 Dionysius explains (*Coel. Hier.* iv, vii). On like manner therefore
the unfolding of faith must needs reach men of lower degree
through those of higher degree. Consequently, just as the higher
angels, who enlighten those who are below them, have a fuller
knowledge of Divine things than the lower angels, as Dionysius
35 states (*Coel. Hier.* xii), so too, men of higher degree, whose
business it is to teach others, are under obligation to have fuller
knowledge of matters of faith, and to believe them more
explicitly.

Reply to Objection 1. The unfolding of the articles of faith
40 is not equally necessary for the salvation of all, since those of
higher degree, whose duty it is to teach others, are bound to
believe explicitly more things than others are.

Reply to Objection 2. Simple persons should not be put to the test about subtle questions of faith, unless they be suspected of having been corrupted by heretics, who are wont to corrupt the faith of simple people in such questions. If, however, it is found
5   that they are free from obstinacy in their heterodox sentiments, and that it is due to their simplicity, it is no fault of theirs.

Reply to Objection 3. The simple have no faith implied in that of the learned, except in so far as the latter adhere to the Divine teaching. Hence the Apostle says (1 Corinthians 4:16): "Be
10   ye followers of me, as I also am of Christ." Hence it is not human knowledge, but the Divine truth that is the rule of faith: and if any of the learned stray from this rule, he does not harm the faith of the simple ones, who think that the learned believe aright; unless the simple hold obstinately to their individual errors, against the
15   faith of the universal Church, which cannot err, since Our Lord said (Luke 22:32): "I have prayed for thee," Peter, "that thy faith fail not."

20   *Article 7. Whether it is necessary for the salvation of all,*
that they should believe explicitly in the mystery of Christ?

Objection 1. It would seem that it is not necessary for the salvation of all that they should believe explicitly in the mystery of
25   Christ. For man is not bound to believe explicitly what the angels are ignorant about: since the unfolding of faith is the result of Divine revelation, which reaches man by means of the angels, as stated above (6; I, 111, 1). Now even the angels were in ignorance of the mystery of the Incarnation: hence, according to
30   the commentary of Dionysius (*Coel. Hier.* vii), it is they who ask (Psalm 23:8): "Who is this king of glory?" and (Isaiah 63:1): "Who is this that cometh from Edom?" Therefore men were not bound to believe explicitly in the mystery of Christ's Incarnation.

Objection 2. Further, it is evident that John the Baptist was
35   one of the teachers, and most nigh to Christ, Who said of him (Matthew 11:11) that "there hath not risen among them that are born of women, a greater than" he. Now John the Baptist does not appear to have known the mystery of Christ explicitly, since he asked Christ (Matthew 11:3): "Art Thou He that art to come, or
40   look we for another?" Therefore even the teachers were not bound to explicit faith in Christ.

Objection 3. Further, many gentiles obtained salvation through the ministry of the angels, as Dionysius states (*Coel. Hier.* ix). Now it would seem that the gentiles had neither explicit nor implicit faith in Christ, since they received no revelation.
5 Therefore it seems that it was not necessary for the salvation of all to believe explicitly in the mystery of Christ.

On the contrary, Augustine says (*De Corr. et Gratia* vii; Ep. cxc): "Our faith is sound if we believe that no man, old or young is delivered from the contagion of death and the bonds of sin, except
10 by the one Mediator of God and men, Jesus Christ."

I answer that, As stated above (5; 1, 8), the object of faith includes, properly and directly, that thing through which man obtains beatitude. Now the mystery of Christ's Incarnation and Passion is the way by which men obtain beatitude; for it is written
15 (Acts 4:12): "There is no other name under heaven given to men, whereby we must be saved." Therefore belief of some kind in the mystery of Christ's Incarnation was necessary at all times and for all persons, but this belief differed according to differences of times and persons. The reason of this is that before the state of sin,
20 man believed, explicitly in Christ's Incarnation, in so far as it was intended for the consummation of glory, but not as it was intended to deliver man from sin by the Passion and Resurrection, since man had no foreknowledge of his future sin. He does, however, seem to have had foreknowledge of the Incarnation of
25 Christ, from the fact that he said (Genesis 2:24): "Wherefore a man shall leave father and mother, and shall cleave to his wife," of which the Apostle says (Ephesians 5:32) that "this is a great sacrament... in Christ and the Church," and it is incredible that the first man was ignorant about this sacrament.

30 But after sin, man believed explicitly in Christ, not only as to the Incarnation, but also as to the Passion and Resurrection, whereby the human race is delivered from sin and death: for they would not, else, have foreshadowed Christ's Passion by certain sacrifices both before and after the Law, the meaning of which
35 sacrifices was known by the learned explicitly, while the simple folk, under the veil of those sacrifices, believed them to be ordained by God in reference to Christ's coming, and thus their knowledge was covered with a veil, so to speak. And, as stated above (Question 1, Article 7), the nearer they were to Christ, the
40 more distinct was their knowledge of Christ's mysteries.

After grace had been revealed, both learned and simple folk are bound to explicit faith in the mysteries of Christ, chiefly as regards

those which are observed throughout the Church, and publicly proclaimed, such as the articles which refer to the Incarnation, of which we have spoken above (Question 1, Article 8). As to other minute points in reference to the articles of the Incarnation, men
5   have been bound to believe them more or less explicitly according to each one's state and office.

Reply to Objection 1. The mystery of the Kingdom of God was not entirely hidden from the angels, as Augustine observes (*Gen. ad lit.* v, 19), yet certain aspects thereof were better known
10   to them when Christ revealed them to them.

Reply to Objection 2. It was not through ignorance that John the Baptist inquired of Christ's advent in the flesh, since he had clearly professed his belief therein, saying: "I saw, and I gave testimony, that this is the Son of God" (John 1:34). Hence he did
15   not say: "Art Thou He that hast come?" but "Art Thou He that art to come?" thus saying about the future, not about the past. Likewise it is not to be believed that he was ignorant of Christ's future Passion, for he had already said (John 1:39): "Behold the Lamb of God, behold Him who taketh away the sins [Vulgate:
20   'sin'] of the world," thus foretelling His future immolation; and since other prophets had foretold it, as may be seen especially in Isaias 53. We may therefore say with Gregory (Hom. xxvi in Evang.) that he asked this question, being in ignorance as to whether Christ would descend into hell in His own Person. But he
25   did not ignore the fact that the power of Christ's Passion would be extended to those who were detained in Limbo, according to Zechariah 9:11: "Thou also, by the blood of Thy testament hast sent forth Thy prisoners out of the pit, wherein there is no water"; nor was he bound to believe explicitly, before its fulfilment, that
30   Christ was to descend thither Himself.

It may also be replied that, as Ambrose observes in his commentary on Luke 7:19, he made this inquiry, not from doubt or ignorance but from devotion: or again, with Chrysostom (Hom. xxxvi in Matth.), that he inquired, not as though ignorant
35   himself, but because he wished his disciples to be satisfied on that point, through Christ: hence the latter framed His answer so as to instruct the disciples, by pointing to the signs of His works.

Reply to Objection 3. Many of the gentiles received revelations of Christ, as is clear from their predictions. Thus we
40   read (Job 19:25): "I know that my Redeemer liveth." The Sibyl too foretold certain things about Christ, as Augustine states (*Contra Faust.* xiii, 15). Moreover, we read in the history of the

Romans, that at the time of Constantine Augustus and his mother
Irene a tomb was discovered, wherein lay a man on whose breast
was a golden plate with the inscription: "Christ shall be born of a
virgin, and in Him, I believe. O sun, during the lifetime of Irene
5 and Constantine, thou shalt see me again" [Cf. *Baron, Annal.*, A.D.
780.] If, however, some were saved without receiving any
revelation, they were not saved without faith in a Mediator, for,
though they did not believe in Him explicitly, they did,
nevertheless, have implicit faith through believing in Divine
10 providence, since they believed that God would deliver mankind
in whatever way was pleasing to Him, and according to the
revelation of the Spirit to those who knew the truth, as stated in
Job 35:11: "Who teacheth us more than the beasts of the earth."

15

Article 8. Whether it is necessary for salvation to believe explicitly in the Trinity?

Objection 1. It would seem that it was not necessary for
20 salvation to believe explicitly in the Trinity. For the Apostle says
(Hebrews 11:6): "He that cometh to God must believe that He is,
and is a rewarder to them that seek Him." Now one can believe
this without believing in the Trinity. Therefore it was not
necessary to believe explicitly in the Trinity.
25 **Objection 2.** Further our Lord said (John 17:5-6): "Father, I
have manifested Thy name to men," which words Augustine
expounds (Tract. cvi) as follows: "Not the name by which Thou
art called God, but the name whereby Thou art called My Father,"
and further on he adds: "In that He made this world, God is
30 known to all nations; in that He is not to be worshipped together
with false gods, 'God is known in Judea'; but, in that He is the
Father of this Christ, through Whom He takes away the sin of the
world, He now makes known to men this name of His, which
hitherto they knew not." Therefore before the coming of Christ it
35 was not known that Paternity and Filiation were in the Godhead:
and so the Trinity was not believed explicitly.
Objection 3. Further, that which we are bound to believe
explicitly of God is the object of heavenly happiness. Now the
object of heavenly happiness is the sovereign good, which can be
40 understood to be in God, without any distinction of Persons.
Therefore it was not necessary to believe explicitly in the Trinity.

On the contrary, In the Old Testament the Trinity of Persons is expressed in many ways; thus at the very outset of Genesis it is written in manifestation of the Trinity: "Let us make man to Our image and likeness" (Genesis 1:26). Therefore from
5   the very beginning it was necessary for salvation to believe in the Trinity.

I answer that, It is impossible to believe explicitly in the mystery of Christ, without faith in the Trinity, since the mystery of Christ includes that the Son of God took flesh; that He renewed
10 the world through the grace of the Holy Ghost; and again, that He was conceived by the Holy Ghost. Wherefore just as, before Christ, the mystery of Christ was believed explicitly by the learned, but implicitly and under a veil, so to speak, by the simple, so too was it with the mystery of the Trinity. And
15 consequently, when once grace had been revealed, all were bound to explicit faith in the mystery of the Trinity: and all who are born again in Christ, have this bestowed on them by the invocation of the Trinity, according to Matthew 28:19: "Going therefore teach ye all nations, baptizing them in the name of the Father, and of the
20 Son and of the Holy Ghost."

Reply to Objection 1. Explicit faith in those two things was necessary at all times and for all people: but it was not sufficient at all times and for all people.

Reply to Objection 2. Before Christ's coming, faith in the
25 Trinity lay hidden in the faith of the learned, but through Christ and the apostles it was shown to the world.

Reply to Objection 3. God's sovereign goodness as we understand it now through its effects, can be understood without the Trinity of Persons: but as understood in itself, and as seen by
30 the Blessed, it cannot be understood without the Trinity of Persons. Moreover the mission of the Divine Persons brings us to heavenly happiness.

35   *Article 9. Whether to believe is meritorious?*

Objection 1. It would seem that to believe in not meritorious. For the principle of all merit is charity, as stated above (I-II, 114, 4). Now faith, like nature, is a preamble to
40 charity. Therefore, just as an act of nature is not meritorious, since we do not merit by our natural gifts, so neither is an act of faith.

Objection 2. Further, belief is a mean between opinion and scientific knowledge or the consideration of things scientifically known [Science is a certain knowledge of a demonstrated conclusion through its demonstration.]. Now the considerations of
5 science are not meritorious, nor on the other hand is opinion. Therefore belief is not meritorious.

Objection 3. Further, he who assents to a point of faith, either has a sufficient motive for believing, or he has not. If he has a sufficient motive for his belief, this does not seem to imply any
10 merit on his part, since he is no longer free to believe or not to believe: whereas if he has not a sufficient motive for believing, this is a mark of levity, according to Sirach 19:4: "He that is hasty to give credit, is light of heart," so that, seemingly, he gains no merit thereby. Therefore to believe is by no means meritorious.

15 **On the contrary,** It is written (Hebrews 11:33) that the saints "by faith . . . obtained promises," which would not be the case if they did not merit by believing. Therefore to believe is meritorious.

I answer that, As stated above (I-II, 114, 3,4), our actions
20 are meritorious in so far as they proceed from the free-will moved with grace by God. Therefore every human act proceeding from the free-will, if it be referred to God, can be meritorious. Now the act of believing is an act of the intellect assenting to the Divine truth at the command of the will moved by the grace of God, so
25 that it is subject to the free-will in relation to God; and consequently the act of faith can be meritorious.

Reply to Objection 1. Nature is compared to charity which is the principle of merit, as matter to form: whereas faith is compared to charity as the disposition which precedes the ultimate
30 form. Now it is evident that the subject or the matter cannot act save by virtue of the form, nor can a preceding disposition, before the advent of the form: but after the advent of the form, both the subject and the preceding disposition act by virtue of the form, which is the chief principle of action, even as the heat of fire acts
35 by virtue of the substantial form of fire. Accordingly neither nature nor faith can, without charity, produce a meritorious act; but, when accompanied by charity, the act of faith is made meritorious thereby, even as an act of nature, and a natural act of the free-will.

40 **Reply to Objection 2.** Two things may be considered in science: namely the scientist's assent to a scientific fact and his consideration of that fact. Now the assent of science is not subject

to free-will, because the scientist is obliged to assent by force of the demonstration, wherefore scientific assent is not meritorious. But the actual consideration of what a man knows scientifically is subject to his free-will, for it is in his power to consider or not to

5   consider. Hence scientific consideration may be meritorious if it be referred to the end of charity, i.e. to the honor of God or the good of our neighbor. On the other hand, in the case of faith, both these things are subject to the free-will so that in both respects the act of faith can be meritorious: whereas in the case of opinion,

10   there is no firm assent, since it is weak and infirm, as the Philosopher observes (*Poster.* i, 33), so that it does not seem to proceed from a perfect act of the will: and for this reason, as regards the assent, it does not appear to be very meritorious, though it can be as regards the actual consideration.

15   **Reply to Objection 3**. The believer has sufficient motive for believing, for he is moved by the authority of Divine teaching confirmed by miracles, and, what is more, by the inward instinct of the Divine invitation: hence he does not believe lightly. He has not, however, sufficient reason for scientific knowledge, hence he

20   does not lose the merit.

Article 10. Whether reasons in support of what we believe lessen the merit of faith?

25

Objection 1. It would seem that reasons in support of what we believe lessen the merit of faith. For Gregory says (Hom. xxvi in Evang.) that "there is no merit in believing what is shown by reason." If, therefore, human reason provides sufficient proof, the

30   merit of faith is altogether taken away. Therefore it seems that any kind of human reasoning in support of matters of faith, diminishes the merit of believing.

Objection 2. Further, whatever lessens the measure of virtue, lessens the amount of merit, since "happiness is the reward of

35   virtue," as the Philosopher states (Ethic. i, 9). Now human reasoning seems to diminish the measure of the virtue of faith, since it is essential to faith to be about the unseen, as stated above (1, 4,5). Now the more a thing is supported by reasons the less is it unseen. Therefore human reasons in support of matters of faith

40   diminish the merit of faith.

Objection 3. Further, contrary things have contrary causes. Now an inducement in opposition to faith increases the merit of faith whether it consist in persecution inflicted by one who endeavors to force a man to renounce his faith, or in an argument persuading him to do so. Therefore reasons in support of faith diminish the merit of faith.

5   **On the contrary**, It is written (1 Peter 3:15): "Being ready always to satisfy every one that asketh you a reason of that faith [Vulgate: 'Of that hope which is in you.' St. Thomas' reading is apparently taken from Bede.] and hope which is in you." Now the Apostle would not give this advice, if it would imply a diminution

10   in the merit of faith. Therefore reason does not diminish the merit of faith.

        I answer that, As stated above (Article 9), the act of faith can be meritorious, in so far as it is subject to the will, not only as to the use, but also as to the assent. Now human reason in support of

15   what we believe, may stand in a twofold relation to the will of the believer. First, as preceding the act of the will; as, for instance, when a man either has not the will, or not a prompt will, to believe, unless he be moved by human reasons: and in this way human reason diminishes the merit of faith. On this sense it has

20   been said above (I-II, 24, 3, ad 1; 77, 6, ad 2) that, in moral virtues, a passion which precedes choice makes the virtuous act less praiseworthy. For just as a man ought to perform acts of moral virtue, on account of the judgment of his reason, and not on account of a passion, so ought he to believe matters of faith, not

25   on account of human reason, but on account of the Divine authority. Secondly, human reasons may be consequent to the will of the believer. For when a man's will is ready to believe, he loves the truth he believes, he thinks out and takes to heart whatever reasons he can find in support thereof; and in this way human

30   reason does not exclude the merit of faith but is a sign of greater merit. Thus again, in moral virtues a consequent passion is the sign of a more prompt will, as stated above (I-II, 24, 3, ad 1). We have an indication of this in the words of the Samaritans to the woman, who is a type of human reason: "We now believe, not for thy

35   saying" (John 4:42).

        Reply to Objection 1. Gregory is referring to the case of a man who has no will to believe what is of faith, unless he be induced by reasons. But when a man has the will to believe what is of faith on the authority of God alone, although he may have

40   reasons in demonstration of some of them, e.g. of the existence of God, the merit of his faith is not, for that reason, lost or diminished.

Reply to Objection 2. The reasons which are brought forward in support of the authority of faith, are not demonstrations which can bring intellectual vision to the human intellect, wherefore they do not cease to be unseen.

5 But they remove obstacles to faith, by showing that what faith proposes is not impossible; wherefore such reasons do not diminish the merit or the measure of faith. On the other hand, though demonstrative reasons in support of the preambles of faith [The Leonine Edition reads: 'in support of matters of faith which

10 are however, preambles to the articles of faith, diminish,' etc.], but not of the articles of faith, diminish the measure of faith, since they make the thing believed to be seen, yet they do not diminish the measure of charity, which makes the will ready to believe them, even if they were unseen; and so the measure of merit is not

15 diminished.

Reply to Objection 3. Whatever is in opposition to faith, whether it consist in a man's thoughts, or in outward persecution, increases the merit of faith, in so far as the will is shown to be more prompt and firm in believing. Hence the martyrs had more

20 merit of faith, through not renouncing faith on account of persecution; and even the wise have greater merit of faith, through not renouncing their faith on account of the reasons brought forward by philosophers or heretics in opposition to faith. On the other hand things that are favorable to faith, do not always

25 diminish the promptness of the will to believe, and therefore they do not always diminish the merit of faith.